©Day One Publications 2010
First printed 2010

Unless otherwise indicated, Scripture quotations are from the New King James Version
(NKJV)®. Copyright © 1982 by Thomas Nelson, Inc. Used by permission. All rights reserved.

A CIP record is held at the British Library

ISBN 978-1-84625-199-3

Published by Day One Publications, Ryelands Road, Leominster, HR6 8NZ
☎ 01568 613 740
FAX 01568 611 473
email—sales@dayone.co.uk
web site—www.dayone.co.uk
North American email—usasales@dayone.co.uk

Cover designed by Wayne McMaster and printed by Orchard Press, Cheltenham Ltd.

Dedicated to the memory of
Sarah Fletcher (1890–1990)
and Gwyneth Jones (1915–1991)

ENDORSEMENTS

James 1:27 is very clear on some of the deeds that need to emanate from a converted heart: a life separated from the corruption of the world and the taking care of orphans and widows. In recent days much has been written about adopting orphans, but little is written specifically for widows and their needs. Here is considerable help and encouragement for widows, as well as important insights for those who minister to them. May Austin Walker's much-needed and welcome application of the numerous passages on widows have a wide circulation!

Dr Michael A. G. Haykin, Professor of Church History and Biblical Spirituality, The Southern Baptist Theological Seminary, Louisville, Kentucky; Director of The Andrew Fuller Center for Baptist Studies; and Research Professor of Irish Baptist College, Constituent College of Queen's University Belfast, N. Ireland

This book will help you. There is nothing better than the counsels you will find here.

Revd Geoff Thomas, Pastor since 1965 of Alfred Place Baptist Church, Aberystwyth, Wales

Does the Bible have much to say by way of precepts and examples concerning God's special care for and commitment to the broken hearts and shattered lives of widows? Do the Scriptures address the church regarding its peculiar responsibilities to be sensitive and caring with respect to the peculiar needs of its widows? Are there clear directives to widows themselves regarding how they may best cope with their widowhood and even use that state as a platform for greater service to Christ and to his people? In this Scripture-soaked book, written out of an experienced and caring pastor's heart, these questions are answered with tenderness and biblical authority. Thank you, Pastor Walker, for giving us a much-needed book.

Albert N. Martin, former pastor of Trinity Baptist Church, Montville, New Jersey, USA; conference speaker; and lecturer in Pastoral Theology

'A widow …' It was always there, way at the back of your mind, the possibility of one day losing your husband, but you had hoped it would be much further away, and that you'd have known a longer time together. Now half of you has died; what you were in this world cannot return. If you are a Christian, you submit to what God has chosen to do, crying to him for grace to receive this grievous providence, knowing that one day the Lord will give a full explanation of your loss to your eternal satisfaction. If you are not a Christian, this is a time to consider again the living God. Is it chance that brought you and your late husband together? Was it luck that led you to wed the one you loved? Do you think, 'It was all chance', or wasn't there a loving Providence that brought you to your dearest? Now would be the best time to find peace with God through Jesus Christ his Son.

I do believe that losing a husband is the greatest loss a woman can experience. Bless God for the memories, for that brave, sweet, loving man God gave you, but now face the challenge of the future as God would have you face it: usefully and wisely, a servant of the family, the church, and the Lord, getting strength day by day from him, that One whom your dearest friend might now be worshipping with all his powers. At God's right hand are pleasures for evermore. Do everything in your power to join him in that place. Soon you too must leave this world. Until that time, may God equip you to live without bitterness in a growing and deepening relationship with our Saviour. This book will help you. There is nothing better than the counsels you will find here, but reading it may yet be too soon, and you are still sensitive. God will help you with that, too. A day will come when you will find it wise and strengthening. Then read it to help yourself, your children, and others. 'Lord, make me usable without my husband. Let me do something for you.'

Revd Geoff Thomas, Pastor since 1965 of Alfred Place Baptist Church, Aberystwyth, Wales

CONTENTS

INTRODUCTION

*Pure and undefiled religion before God and the Father
is this: to visit orphans and widows in their trouble,
and to keep oneself unspotted from the world.*

James 1:27

Faith is more than mere words. It must display itself in works if it is genuine. James is not sounding an isolated note when he speaks about visiting 'orphans and widows in their trouble' as being one of those works that is evidence of real faith. It is a note that resounds again and again throughout the entirety of Scripture, from the days of Moses to those of the apostles and the early church.

God, the Redeemer of Israel, repeatedly declared that widows (along with the fatherless and the stranger) are the special object of his concern and love (see, e.g., Exod. 22:22–24). The prophets of the old covenant rebuked those who oppressed widows, and placed such oppression alongside the sins of murder and idolatry (see Jer. 7:5–6).

Our Lord Jesus Christ pronounced a solemn woe on the hypocrisy of the scribes and Pharisees on the basis that 'you devour widows' houses' (Matt. 23:14). In the temple he pointed out the widow who threw two mites into the treasury, commending her because 'she out of her poverty put in all she had' (Mark 12:44). Even in his hour of deepest distress on the cross he did not forget his own widowed mother, commending her to the care of John (John 19:26–27). The apostles, when threatened with a dispute over the care of the widows in the church in Jerusalem, were careful to appoint no fewer than seven well-qualified men, full of the Holy Spirit, in order to ensure that unity in the church was maintained and that no widow was neglected (Acts 6:1–6). Paul urged Timothy at Ephesus to 'Honor widows who are really widows' (1 Tim. 5:3).

It is still the task of the church to 'visit orphans and widows in their trouble'. This book is largely the result of my attempts, over a period of some thirty or more years, to comfort widows in their varied distresses. The only book I could find during those years was *The Widow Directed to the Widow's God* by John Angell James. While it contained a lot of helpful counsel, it was dated. I decided to go back and study the Scriptures. I was amazed to discover just how close the widow's troubles are to the heart of God himself, and I therefore became troubled by the fact that, too often, the needs of the widow are forgotten. It is out of those same Scriptures that I have sought to minister comfort to those widows whom 'the Father of mercies and God of all comfort' (2 Cor. 1:3) has brought into the church.

This explains why the book is dedicated to the memory of two noble ladies. Sarah Fletcher was approaching her eightieth year and had been a widow for a number of years when I first met her. Her father had been prominent in politics in Nottingham and had been the first Lord Mayor of the city in 1929. Many years later, in 1962, and now widowed, she moved from Nottingham to Crawley in order to be cared for by her daughter and family. Her first real interest in the gospel began when she was in her seventies, when she heard Dr Martyn Lloyd-Jones preach in Westminster Chapel, London. The seed that was sown in her heart was watered when she began to attend Cuckfield Baptist Chapel in West Sussex. When, in the early 1970s, she attended the church in Crawley that was planted by Cuckfield, she was converted to Christ. She was baptized at the age of eighty-three and became a founder-member of the newly formed Crawley Reformed Baptist Church in 1975. From that point on, until her death in 1990—three months short of her hundredth birthday—it was my privilege to preach to her each Lord's Day and then, as old age overtook her and confined her to her home, to visit her regularly. It was only then that I, as a young and relatively inexperienced pastor, began to enter into her world as a widow—into her sorrows and her joys. Only then did I begin to understand a little of what it meant to bring the compassion and love of God to bear on her troubles.

Gwyneth Jones was very different. Living in Rhigos, a farming community close to the Brecon Beacons in South Wales, she had turned against the church, put off by the religious hypocrisy she had observed in the church of her youth. Having married in 1938, she and her husband, William, had two children. Tragically, her husband was killed in a motorcycle accident in 1950. She was plunged into poverty and distress, suffering two mental breakdowns. In 1971, I married Mai, who was her daughter. Very independent but increasingly vulnerable, living alone in a socially deprived housing estate in Penywaun, near Aberdare, Gwyneth Jones eventually came to live in Crawley so that we could care for her in her declining years. By now she was hard of hearing, but also hardened in her heart and very sceptical about the truth of the gospel of Christ. She trusted hardly anyone at all. Over a period of years I spent many hours with her, explaining the Bible. She would not come to church on any regular basis. She was nervous of meeting people and would sit at the back and disappear as soon as the service was over so that she did not have to talk to anyone. Gradually she warmed to the truth of the gospel and God was pleased to open her eyes and give her faith in Christ. By this time, she had contracted cancer; at one point, before she had come to faith, the doctors had given up hope of preserving her life. The church prayed earnestly and the Lord spared her life for a few more years, during which time she professed her new-found faith in Christ. This was mingled with words of deep regret: 'Oh, I should have done this many years ago!' A few months later in 1991, she fell asleep in Christ.

As with Sarah Fletcher, to visit this needy widow and also to bring to her the saving knowledge of Christ was a learning experience that no book on pastoral theology could ever have taught me. Since then it has been my task to minister to other ladies who have become widows. Among them is Sarah Fletcher's own daughter, Margaret Smith, who has been a faithful lifetime member of the church in which I minister.

What follows in this book is written in the hope that what I have learned from the Word of God will be a means of bringing comfort and help to other widows in their distress. In no way do I consider myself an expert. I have simply sought to be a pastor to those needy sheep that the Head of the church has been pleased to make a part of his flock, and to bring something of the comfort that God himself is to his own people.

While *God's Care for the Widow* is written primarily for the Christian widow, I hope it will also be read by those who are not yet Christians. My prayer is that, with God's blessing, the book may become a means of bringing them to trust in God. God has many different ways of drawing sinners to Christ. Sometimes God deliberately brings 'trouble' and sorrows into our lives. However, he then uses those experiences by his mercy and grace to soften our hearts and to show us the emptiness of the world and the foolishness of our lives lived without him. By these means he then draws us to see that we are sinners in need of the Saviour, the Lord Jesus Christ. Sarah Fletcher and Gwyneth Jones were not Christians when their husbands died, yet both ladies eventually came to know the God who became their 'refuge and strength, a very present help in trouble' (Ps. 46:1). They found a happiness and security in God that could not be found in any human relationship.

This book can be used in different ways. It can be read through from cover to cover, or it can be used on a daily basis, taking one brief chapter at a time. Sometimes, perhaps in a time of extreme sorrow, one such chapter each day will prove to be sufficient. It may not be the right book to pick up when experiencing that time of intense shock and confusion that invariably follows the death of a loved one; however, the book is written in the hope that it will prove to be helpful in the process of adjustment that must subsequently take place sooner or later. Everyone is different, and the process of grief varies according to the individual widow and her circumstances. I also hope that the book will prove to be a helpful guide to other pastors who are called to minister to widows in their own congregations and on a wider front.

Someone might ask, 'What about the widower? What does God's Word say to him in his grief and sorrow?' Abraham mourned and wept for his Sarah (Gen. 23:2). The godly Andrew Bonar recorded in his diary the abiding grief he experienced as a result of the loss of his Isabella, his wife of seventeen years, referring to her on each anniversary of her death.[1] Many of the biblical principles which I seek to apply to widows in the following pages apply equally to the widower. On the other hand, the Bible deals with strangers, orphans and widows as 'a special case' because of their greater vulnerability. For that reason I have chosen in this book to focus on the widow.

For widowers, I would recommend Donald Howard's booklet *Christians Grieve Too*.[2] Mr Howard wrote his booklet after the death of his first wife from cancer. He found himself ill-prepared to cope with grief. Writing from his personal experience, he also writes as a pastor, with valuable biblical insights. Widowers may also find C. S. Lewis's *A Grief Observed* a help, as did Donald Howard.[3] More recently, Albert N. Martin preached three sermons, *Gleanings from a Grieving Heart*, which were delivered a few weeks after the death of his wife in September 2004.[4] Each of these men provides very helpful counsel for anyone who is facing grief.

Chapter 1

A defender of widows

A father of the fatherless, a
defender of widows,
Is God in His holy habitation.
Psalm 68:5

A widow is the special object of God's concern and love. God dwells in the highest heaven, his holy dwelling place, yet his eye watches all that happens here on earth and focuses not least on the widow in her particular troubles. He himself said so when he revealed himself in the Scriptures as the 'defender of widows'.

When David was in trouble, hotly pursued by Saul, he appealed to God in his righteousness as a judge: 'let the LORD be judge, and judge between you and me, and see and plead my case, and deliver me out of your hand' (1 Sam. 24:15). God as the righteous judge or defender is the one who sees the issues clearly and pleads the cause of the needy. He is the advocate of those who are vulnerable and exposed to injustice. God calls on his people to defend the case of widows, but he is their ultimate defender. When a widow is wronged, he who dwells in heaven, who makes the clouds his chariot, sees and takes note, and his anger is aroused against those who have ill-treated her. He quickly rises to her defence.

The parable of the unjust judge in Luke 18:1–8 drives home the same point. The Lord Jesus relates how a widow came before a judge who 'did not fear God nor regard man'. She was being oppressed: someone was taking advantage of her in her position as a widow, and so she pleaded with the judge for justice. In the end, wearied by her persistence, the unjust judge decided to defend her cause. Although Christ has a broader application than the widow's situation, the implication is clear. Our Lord teaches us that God is not like the unjust judge, slow and reluctant to help. On the contrary, he is quick to see and to defend all his elect who cry out day and night to him. The widow who trusts in God is not excluded.

Widows are to draw encouragement from this and should not be slow in crying out to their advocate, their righteous judge and defender. In Scripture they are invariably found crying out to God in heaven as the one who sees, as the one who will righteously plead their case. The sorrows and griefs of widowhood invariably instil doubts and fears into the heart. The sense of loss is shattering. It shakes them in the very core of their being. Doubts about God's care arise. Fears about the future set off a train of anxieties. Seemingly endless tears of distress may flow from their eyes. They now find themselves in a vulnerable situation.

Has God abandoned the widow? Is she now alone in her grief? Has her Father in heaven forgotten her and cut her off from his compassion? Satan is not slow to inject such thoughts into a widow's mind. Yet the Lord is quick to rise to her defence and protect her from Satan's malice and human wrongdoing. His mercies are intended to draw her to him; even more so her grief and her troubles. They are intended to drive her into his arms to find safety and security in him, and to prove him to be the righteous defender of her case. He is a true Father, one who does not shun the tears of any of his distressed children, nor shut his ears to their cries.

The verse from Psalm 68 that speaks of God as 'a defender of widows' declares to us that we have a gracious God, a sovereign God full of mercy and tender compassion. He is great, dwelling in glory in heaven. But he condescends to use his greatness and power to come to the aid of the needy, to protect them in their vulnerability. That is the kind of God he is—mighty and merciful. The fatherless, the widow, and the lonely will discover that this God is totally sufficient for their needs. When families experience bereavement and lose their beloved head, this God takes care of them. *He* becomes their shield and protector. If you are a widow, therefore, he will act on your behalf. As you come to him in prayer, lay hold of him in his capacity as your defender.

This means that his ear will always be open to your cries and his hand open for all your needs. He will not and cannot abandon you, because by so doing he would deny himself to be the very God he repeatedly declares himself to be. You therefore have freedom to come to him and to call on him as your heavenly Father and your righteous judge and defender. He will bless you, he will teach you, and he will comfort you in your grief. He will listen sympathetically to your grievances and he will plead your cause. He will stand up for you and own you as his needy one whom he delights to defend. Happy is the widow who has this God for her help!

Chapter 2

God relieves the widow

The LORD watches over the strangers;
He relieves the fatherless and widow;
But the way of the wicked
He turns upside down.
Psalm 146:9

In the ancient pagan world, becoming a widow was the fate most feared by a woman. To lose your protector and provider was regarded as the worst thing that could happen to you. The word 'widow' is probably derived from a root word that means 'forsaken', 'left empty', or 'desolate'. The gods of antiquity were regarded as powerless, unable to help widows. Today, when death removes a husband, fear, despair, and helplessness often set in. Then, all too often, the religious and moral bankruptcy of our twenty-first-century world is horribly exposed. However, those who trust in God are to be different. In the Scriptures God is portrayed as the one who relieves or sustains the widow.

In the Old Testament the legal plight of the widow was often one of the main problems she faced. It was hard for her to get justice. Often she would find herself held in very low esteem by others, and her needs were neglected. The care and concern of God was reflected in a number of different commandments that he gave to the nation of Israel and which were intended to make provision for widows and to sustain them. For example, a widow's garment was never to be taken as a pledge (Deut. 24:17). Or again, the gleanings of the grain, olive, and grape harvests were to be left for the stranger, the fatherless, and the widow (Deut. 24:19–21). Widows were not to be excluded from the Feast of Weeks (Deut. 16:11) and were expected to eat and to enjoy the blessings that God had brought to the nation from the 'tithe of [their] increase in the third year' (Deut. 26:12–13). In these various ways God provided relief for the widow and thus maintained her well-being and sustained her life.

But he also relieved the widow when she was being unkindly treated. 'You shall not afflict any widow or fatherless child. If you afflict them in any way, and they cry at all to Me, I will surely hear their cry' (Exod. 22:22–23). God does not show partiality. He does not pay attention to the rich and well-dressed and treat the poor and needy with contempt (see James 2:1–4). He cannot be bribed like men; 'He administers justice for the fatherless and the widow, and loves the stranger, giving him food and clothing' (Deut. 10:18). He establishes 'the boundary of the widow' (Prov. 15:25). Anyone moving a boundary stone marking out the land owned by a widow (or any other Israelite) was guilty of theft. God denounced this evil and warned Israel that he would use his power against such an underhand thief and come to the widow's defence (see Prov. 23:10–11). This kind of protection was also a means of relief for the widow.

It is easy to miss the reason God gave for the provision for and relief of widows. He does not speak and give commandments to the people of God without good reasons. Israel had once experienced 'trouble' in Egypt. They had been afflicted. As slaves they had endured hard bondage. As strangers in the land of Egypt they had been ill-treated. Worn down by this oppression they had groaned, but the Lord heard their groaning (Exod. 2:23–24). He came to their aid and redeemed them. Now they were to show to those in trouble the same kind of love and concern which they themselves had experienced from the hand of God (Exod. 22:21; Deut. 24:18, 22). The Lord said that this included showing love to and concern for the widows among them, ensuring that they were not neglected or ill-treated.

Psalm 146:9 tells us that the Lord 'relieves' the widow. This means that he helps and sustains her in her great loss.

He is the very one who, as the righteous King, executes 'justice for the oppressed' and 'gives food to the hungry' (v. 7). Thus he comes to the aid of the widow who is vulnerable and weak, and stands between her and those who would ignore or harm her. Let the widow, then, humbly cast herself upon her God, for the Scriptures say, 'The LORD lifts up the humble; He casts the wicked down to the ground' (Ps. 147:6).[1] Thus he both makes provision for the widow and protects her.

There is a thread that runs through all these commandments concerning the relief and protection of widows. What unites them is the character of God himself. He abounds in goodness, kindness, and mercy. His eyes are always open to see the plight of widows and his ears always hear their cries. He is indeed the one who is ready, not only to show his power to defend the widow and to protect her in her vulnerability, but also to come to her aid and relieve her in all her needs. The precise means by which God sustains the widow may be different today, but the character of God has not changed.

As bees collect and store up pollen to turn into honey, so 'Wise people store up knowledge' (Prov. 10:14a). As a widow, you will need to store up this knowledge of God's character and make good use of it so that it becomes pleasant to your taste. When Satan tempts you to despair and plays on your fears, telling you that God would never have allowed you to become a widow if he really loved you, you must ward off the devil's lies with the sword of the Spirit that the Lord puts into your hand—the Word of God (Eph. 6:17). Satan invariably assails the character of God. That is how he enticed Eve. Do not let him ensnare you in a similar fashion.

Go back over these commandments and take heart. However you may feel, it is still your responsibility as a Christian to trust in your heavenly Father's kindness. Lie down as you would in a bath and soak yourself in his goodness and love, and in his provision and protection for you. Reflect on his commandments. They are effectively God's promises to you as a widow, displaying his love and his willingness to relieve you. Has he not committed himself to provide for you, to come to your help precisely at the point where you are vulnerable? We shall consider some of the ways in which God sends relief in later chapters. Sadly, you will probably discover that even good friends fail you. Unlike you, they become forgetful of your grief and fears after a while and sometimes become unfeeling and insensitive. The Lord, on the other hand, has given commandments and made promises. Will he forget his own word? Will he forget you? If he does either of these things he ceases to be God.

Therefore, do not be slow to take your cause to heaven's throne, where God will bend his sympathetic ear. Learn to rely on his revealed character as the one who relieves widows. If you are reading this but not yet trusting God, then I urge you to understand the character and the heart of God towards widows. Perhaps you have never thought of God in this way before, or you were inclined to think that God took no notice of you. Here is a starting point on the way to discovering how this same God can relieve you in your grief.

Chapter 3

Three funerals and three widows

Then Elimelech, Naomi's husband, died; and she was left, and her two sons. Now they took wives of the women of Moab: the name of the one was Orpah, and the name of the other Ruth ... Then both Mahlon and Chilion also died; so the woman survived her two sons and her husband.
Ruth 1:3–5

Examples always help us to understand the ways by which God works in our lives, especially in times of trouble. When Elimelech and his wife, Naomi, with their two sons, Mahlon and Chilion, left Bethlehem for Moab, all appeared to be well. They thought that they would be free of the famine that raged through their homeland. Naomi knew nothing of the troubles that were to dominate her life for the next ten years or so. All seemed to be going smoothly until tragedy struck the family. Her husband died. She was plunged into acute sorrow. Scripture, with much feeling, says 'she was left' (Ruth 1:3). At least she had her two sons. No doubt she found some comfort in her grief when her sons married and she found refuge in one of their homes. Can you imagine, then, how her sorrows were multiplied when first Mahlon and then Chilion died? She felt the intense pain of three funerals. Now Naomi was the lone survivor. What were her prospects as a widow among the Moabites? She naturally expected that her two daughters-in-law would return to their mothers' houses. Then she would be really destitute, and, even worse, she was an Israelite now living in a foreign and ungodly land. How much worse could it get?

Naomi's case may have been extreme but it is not difficult to imagine the nature of her trouble. The word 'trouble' (as used by James in James 1:27) basically refers to 'distress' and to sufferings brought about by the pressure and change of circumstances. The frequency with which Scripture speaks of a widow's 'trouble' suggests that, when a woman's circumstances change and she becomes a widow, she faces far more pressures than a widower.

The death of a husband leaves a widow with an overwhelming sense of destitution, of isolation and emptiness. There is a peculiar pathos in those words describing Naomi—'she was left'. Her life was seemingly torn to shreds. When death took her husband Naomi lost her earthly protector and provider, her best friend, and her earthly companion. She was shaken in the very depths of her being. That is why her grief was so intense.

If your husband was a Christian he was your companion, your comforter, your lover, and your spiritual confidant. But now the one on whom you have come to depend for so much is no longer at your side. At your wedding you undertook to remain husband and wife 'till death do us part', and now that terrible moment which perhaps you never dared to think about has become a permanent reality. Perhaps it came suddenly and much sooner than you anticipated. Perhaps you have young or difficult children to bring up on your own. You had little or no idea what that phrase 'till death do us part' might mean. Its significance was hardly contemplated by you on that happy day.

Others may have enjoyed a much longer life together. You have happy memories: adapting to being a wife, becoming a mother, seeing the children grow up and perhaps marry, and then together rejoicing in your children's children. You grew old together. Together you came through several life-threatening situations as a result of some severe illness. At times it was 'touch and go' but, because of God's goodness to you, you came through those crises together. Perhaps your husband died after a long illness and you did everything you could to care for him while he remained alive. It was a trying as well as a demanding experience.

None of those former crises compare with this new trouble. You are faced with the most difficult change of all and you feel overtaken by a sense of helplessness. You are now alone, vulnerable, and feeling at a complete loss. How will you cope now you are living on your own? Who will do those repair jobs around the home? Who will sort out the household budget and the bills? Sometimes you may wake up in the night and reach out your hand, only to be reminded that the other side of the bed is now cold and empty. There may be times when you may think you see your husband or hear his voice. You feel stupid and reproach yourself, and are reduced again to tears. I recall a similar experience after my father died. Walking into my mother's living room for the first time since his funeral, I began to give my customary greeting to my stroke-bound father sitting in his chair. Grief overwhelmed me. Realizing my 'mistake', I collapsed sobbing into the nearest chair.

Death has come as an intruder and has robbed you of your closest friend. Life will never be the same again. Self-pity threatens to engulf you. You may begin to question the wisdom and kindness of God towards you. You know you ought not to do so, but you find you can scarcely help yourself. Naomi found her changed circumstances very hard to bear and even altered her name: 'Do not call me Naomi; call me Mara, for the Almighty has dealt very bitterly with me' (Ruth 1:20).

If Naomi had no idea of the troubles she was about to face when she left with her family for Moab, she certainly had no inkling of the blessings that God was going to bring to her in her widowhood. She did not remarry but she came to know dimensions of God's love and provision for her and for her daughter-in-law Ruth that were beyond all her expectations. A widow's troubles are particular troubles, but none of them separate her from the goodness of God.

Learning to submit to his will and continuing to believe that no aspect of God has changed despite the changes in your circumstances is now one of your main responsibilities. We will return to this in a later chapter. Such submission is never the work of one day. Naomi struggled. Satan will try to suggest that God has changed and has been unkind to you in removing your husband. Resist him and his wicked insinuations. Rather, trust in God's Word. Remember, God says he is the defender of widows. He has also promised to relieve you. Perhaps he is about to prove himself to you in ways you, like Naomi, could never have imagined. God's providence has placed you now in a realm of sorrow and tears. But is he not good and wise in his providence? Does he not have the right to do with us as he sees best? Is he not good and loving? He is never a harsh Father who takes pleasure in afflicting any of his children.

Your troubles bring a sense of helplessness but not

hopelessness. You may want to give way to your feelings and indulge in self-pity, but your feelings are to be governed by the truth about God made effective in your heart by the power of his Spirit. In your helplessness, cast yourself on God. Self-pity will drive you away from God. Rather, let your troubles drive you into his arms, not away from him.

Like a wise physician he is able to pour oil into your troubled soul, bind up your broken heart, and heal your sorrows. 'For in the time of trouble He shall hide me in His pavilion; in the secret place of His tabernacle He shall hide me; He shall set me high upon a rock' (Ps. 27:5). But that healing will not take place in one day. Nevertheless, he is your heavenly protector and provider, and you are entering into a new experience of God's all-sufficiency and tender compassion. You will find him adequate for all your needs every single day. Trust in him, for he will never fail you. Seek comfort from his Holy Spirit and from the promises of his Word. Pray for his grace to enable you to rest in him, submitting to his wise ways. There you will find that peace 'which surpasses all understanding' (Phil. 4:7) which God alone gives you in Christ Jesus.

Chapter 4

God's bottle for your tears

How lonely sits the city
That was full of people!
How like a widow is she …
She weeps bitterly in the night,
Her tears are on her cheeks.
Lamentations 1:1–2

Tears are part of the way we express our grief. It is not difficult to imagine the sore weeping eyes of Naomi and Ruth. There is nothing shameful when you shed tears because of the bitter sorrow you feel in your innermost being. You may be embarrassed by the experience at first, especially when it happens unexpectedly in public.

When Christ stood at the tomb of Lazarus tears must have flowed down his cheeks. We simply read, 'Jesus wept' (John 11:35). Everyone present saw his tears but he felt no embarrassment. We read in verse 33 that when he saw Mary and her friends weeping there was no rebuke, no disparaging of their grief, even though he was about to raise Lazarus from the dead.

When there is good reason for tears we do not need to apologize to anyone for them. Sadly, others sometimes frown on us for such expressions of grief or have no idea of the depth of feeling that produces such tears. Christ never does this. There is therefore no reason for shame. Christians are commanded to 'Rejoice with those who rejoice, and weep with those who weep' (Rom. 12:15). Yet when it comes to weeping with a widow, some members of the church, or even of the widow's own family, may not be sure how to show compassion and enter into her sorrows. It is all too easy to forget the tears of widows. Some years ago I preached at a conference for pastors. As part of that sermon I mentioned some of the things that ought to be prominent in the public prayers of the church. A few months later I met one of the pastors who had attended the conference and he told me how he now included prayers for widows when he led the congregation in prayer. The first time he had done so, an elderly widow came up to him and told him that this was the only occasion when she had ever heard a pastor pray publicly for widows. Surely that ought never to have been the case!

To grieve with tears is part of how God made us as human beings, and thus grief is a legitimate emotion. Perhaps you have lost your husband and your grief is magnified because you know he was not a Christian. It is right to grieve over him in that situation. The Lord Jesus grieved and wept as he contemplated Jerusalem in her continued unbelief (Luke 19:41–44; Matt. 23:37–39). (Later, we shall consider what comfort the Bible gives us in such circumstances.) Here, though, the Lord teaches us that tears are a genuine expression of and outlet for our sorrow. That is why we find David speaking of God putting 'my tears into Your bottle' (Ps. 56:8). At the time, David was under great pressure from his enemies and in his fear he learned to trust in God. What comforted David in these circumstances? It was the fact that God took particular note of all his grief. God has a bottle for his people's tears. This means that he looks down on you with compassion and tenderness. It means that he is afflicted in your afflictions. The death of his saints is precious in his sight, and so are your tears. Not one tear falls to the ground that does not collect in his bottle. Remember, he heard the groans of his people in Egypt and came to their aid (Exod. 2:24). He had pity on King Hezekiah when he was sick and near death. Isaiah went to him and told him, 'Thus says the LORD ... "I have heard your prayer, I have seen your tears; surely I will heal you"' (2 Kings 20:5).

Your sorrowful state as a widow is no different. In Lamentations Jeremiah described the state of afflicted Jerusalem as 'lonely ... like a widow' (Lam. 1:1). The city had been destroyed and its inhabitants had been taken into exile in Babylon. Jeremiah, often referred to as the weeping prophet (see Jer. 9:1), was overwhelmed with sorrow and grief. The solitary desolation of the widow bereaved of her husband is expressed in sighs and weeping like that of Jerusalem in her affliction. The pain, and the wound that causes the pain, break out in bitter weeping in the night and 'tears are on her cheeks' (1:2).

Note also that these are tears shed in the darkness of night when the intensity of the loneliness is felt more acutely. These are not just the tears shed at the funeral, nor the tears shed among sympathetic friends; they are also the tears shed alone, at night. Others are sleeping but you are wide awake; your thoughts are on your troubles, and the sobs and tears flow and keep on flowing. Perhaps you find yourself groaning before God in your sobbing. At such times when there is no human being to provide comfort, it is good to remember that the God who never slumbers nor sleeps is well aware of your tears and he is putting them once again into his bottle. Only such thoughts of God's mercy and love can provide any relief, calm, and comfort during times of bitterness and desolation.

A word of caution is necessary at this point. If you read on in Lamentations you will soon discover that Jerusalem's sorrows were due to her sin and the judgement of God on that city and the nation of Judah. This is not to suggest that you have been widowed as a judgement of

God. Jeremiah simply likened the loneliness of that city to the loneliness that a widow experiences on the death of her husband. It would be wrong to press the comparison any further.

Many tears of the widow are shed in private. The first year of widowhood is especially hard-going as anniversaries and birthdays come round. A visit to your grandchildren may be especially painful as you learn to go alone and perhaps tell them why grandpa is not with you. Sorrow may overcome you at that time because your husband is not there to enjoy these moments with you. You recall the things you used to do together with them and it pulls you apart once again. Particularly painful will be the anniversary of your husband's death and perhaps of the illness that preceded it, or the memory of the suddenness of it. You will relive these events again and again. Memories of things you did together reopen the wound that you thought was beginning to heal. Fresh tears are invariably shed.

It is tempting in those kinds of circumstances to think, 'No one understands what I am going through.' That is a lie of the devil. Do not believe it, not even for a moment. Surely he who stood weeping at the grave of Lazarus understands your grief. Has he lost the bottle in which he stores his people's tears? Has he forgotten to be compassionate? Like Jeremiah, he mourned and wept over Jerusalem in her spiritual desolation. He knew, too, what it was to grieve in Gethsemane, just a few hours before his death. We read of his desolation, of this 'Man of sorrows ... acquainted with grief' (Isa. 53:3). But he did more than experience grief. He went to the cross and offered himself up as a sacrifice for our sins in order to secure our salvation. From Jesus Christ we receive the forgiveness of sins and the gift of eternal life. He was never more alone than when he cried out from the cross as he endured that profound awareness of being forsaken by God.

The person who truly believes on Christ has been joined to Christ by faith. Christ is alive and as our High Priest he now lives to intercede for us. We must remember that he shared our earthly experiences, including grief, suffering, and death. Therefore he is now able to sympathize with us. Tears on your cheeks, the evidence of bitter weeping in the night, are no exception. He always understands.

He will hear your cry, and you will discover that the more you learn to pour out your heart to Jesus Christ, the more peace and contentment in God you will know, even in the midst of tears. That is a spiritual rule of his kingdom. Do you remember Philippians 4:6–7? 'Be anxious for nothing, but in everything by prayer and supplication, with thanksgiving, let your requests be made known to God; *and the peace of God*, which surpasses all understanding, *will guard your hearts and minds through Christ Jesus*' (emphasis added). Remember also the man who wrote this. A few verses later Paul tells us, '... for I have learned in whatever state I am, to be content' (4:11). Your tears do not make you an exception to experiencing that contentment that comes from pouring out your heart to God.

Chapter 5

Submitting to God's wise ways

Why do you call me Naomi, since
the LORD has testified against me,
and the Almighty has afflicted me?
Ruth 1:21

Let us now return to Naomi's story. 'Mrs Mara' thought that she had been deserted and rejected by God. Her experience had soured her and produced hard thoughts of God. She was persuaded that he was responsible for her bitter distress. She was very quick to kill the excitement of the women who came to meet her on her return to Bethlehem after ten years in exile. She told them firmly, 'Do not call me Naomi [which means "pleasant"]; call me Mara ["bitter"], for the Almighty has dealt very bitterly with me. I went out full, and the LORD has brought me home again empty. Why do you call me Naomi, since the LORD has testified against me, and the Almighty has afflicted me?' (Ruth 1:20–21). She was convinced that, far from being the defender of widows, the Lord had acted against her as if she had been found guilty and been punished. And she had no idea what he had against her!

We can begin to understand her emotional response. She had reached the end of her tether. She was suffering grief and mental anguish, and she expressed a deep-seated spirit of bitterness, a mixture of fear, anger, and frustration, mingled with self-pity. This situation had been building up over the years. She had been in exile in Moab. There she had experienced three funerals. Poverty was her lot; there was no one to provide for her. With no remaining men in the family there were no heirs to perpetuate the name of her husband and her sons. She stood to lose her family inheritance that the Lord had given to her and every other Israelite family. She felt quite helpless and had told her two daughters-in-law as much. The facts stared them all in the face. Naomi was too old to have any more children, and even if she married immediately and had sons, would Ruth and Orpah wait until these sons were old enough to marry? 'Turn back, my daughters ... go,' was the only counsel she could give them (1:11–13).

It is not unusual for a widow to experience anger and self-pity alongside her grief and her fears. Naomi was protesting against God. She felt that he was giving her a raw deal. She was evidently struggling to come to terms with God's ways. She was questioning God's wisdom and his goodness towards her. After all, she had gone out full, but he was the one who brought her home empty! 'Why did Elimelech die just when I needed him most?' Words like these are frequently heard from the lips of grieving widows. They soon produce self-pity. Such attitudes need to be faced and drawn out, if necessary, by a sensitive and understanding pastor or close friend, then discussed and dealt with, if they are going to be eventually removed and replaced by a spirit of submission and contentment.

Such anger and self-pity is understandable but should never be allowed to become the settled pattern. How can such attitudes and feelings be overcome? Godly submission is the only way to quieten the mind and silence the protests on your lips. It is Christ who has removed your husband from you. No Christian doubts that God can bring us to heaven by leading us along an easier, smoother path, should he desire to do so. However, if his providence and wisdom take a different and much more difficult track, it is not for us to summon God to give an account to us of his ways. Like Job, we cannot get to the bottom of his ways (Job 23:8–10). All we see are the broken links in the chain of providence. God has a reason for your troubles, but the fact that you cannot understand what he is doing is no reason to protest against him. Submission, however, is not simply accepting what has happened because there is nothing you can do to change the situation; that is a form of fatalism. Rather, your part is to wait on God, to believe in him and trust in his wisdom, to be confident of his goodness and love, to submit to his will, and to prove his faithfulness and ability to keep you in the storm. Let your trust in God and patience be seen. It was John Newton who wrote in one of his hymns, 'With Christ in the vessel, I smile at the storm.'[1]

None of this minimizes the fact that bereavement tears us apart. It jars every bone in our bodies, and profoundly affects every thought and feeling as well as our conduct. It leaves an aching void and in many cases produces physical pain.

So many of the trials and difficulties we face are connected with our deepest longings, feelings, and affections. Naomi was a wife and a mother, but now she was widowed. Her sons had died too, and her future looked very bleak. Her distinctive feminine sensitivities and feelings were profoundly affected. God's dealings with her affected her health, her emotions, and her sense of security. No wonder she felt as if God was attacking her. She felt distraught in her inner being, to the very depths of her femininity. She probably said things like, 'It isn't just for God to deal with me in this way.' She may have repeatedly asked, 'What has God got against me that he has sent this trouble on me?' God, on the other hand, was intent on sanctifying her in the deepest parts of her womanhood and bringing her to a new appreciation of his all-sufficiency by providing for her.

Naomi and her daughter-in-law Ruth came to learn that God is the kind of God who cares for the widow. He is a true and wise Father. He who made us male and female understands the needs and emotions of women as well as men. Where can a Christian widow learn submission to the will of God? It is by learning from our Saviour. No one understands submission to the will of God better than God's own Son, who endured the dark horrors of Gethsemane and the pain and shame of crucifixion at Golgotha. He experienced the curse and wrath of God as he died on the cross. Naomi only *thought* God had forsaken her. Our Saviour cried out, 'My God, My God, why have You forsaken Me?' (Mark 15:34).

However hard your situation may be, there is one who is really able to sympathize with you in your destitution and in the resulting sense of insecurity and vulnerability. It is none other than Jesus, the Son of God, our great High Priest, full of pity and power. In a later chapter we will consider his compassion in greater detail.

Ruth and Naomi obtained mercy and found refuge under the wings of the Lord God of Israel. In his mercy God provided Boaz as a husband for Ruth. Ruth bore a son, Obed, and that son proved to be 'a restorer of life' and 'a nourisher' of Naomi's old age (Ruth 4:15). Naomi and Ruth came to realize that when God takes away our earthly joys and securities and plunges us into grief, it is in order that we might learn to take refuge under his protective wings and experience his power, his love, his provision, and his sufficiency for all our needs.

God will not deal with you precisely in the same way that he dealt with Naomi and Ruth, but he is still the same God of power and love, and he will never fail you. On returning to Bethlehem, Naomi began a new and different life in very changed circumstances from those she had experienced when her husband was alive. It took Naomi time but, apart from the joy that Ruth brought her, she now had a new son-in-law, and, in due course, her first grandson, Obed. Much of her time initially was spent caring for him.

God will help you to begin a new life as a widow, perhaps opening up new and different ways for you to serve Christ in his church; ways that were not open to you in the past. Godly submission is needed, however, if your wound is to be slowly healed and if you are to understand and accept that it is God who has sent these troubles.

Chapter 6

Joy before the Lord

You shall rejoice before the LORD your God, you and your son and your daughter, your male servant and your female servant, the Levite who is within your gates, the stranger and the fatherless and the widow who are among you, at the place where the LORD your God chooses to make His name abide.
Deuteronomy 16:11

Joy is perhaps the last thing you would associate with being a widow. Weeping and sorrow, yes, but not joy! You can perhaps give a hundred and one reasons why you could not possibly be glad.

Loneliness can be a real problem. Winter months with their long hours of darkness may become especially depressing. Depending on your circumstances, you could end up seeing no one for several days. If your husband was heavily involved in the life of your local church, you may suddenly find yourself cut off from many things you once did together. This will be especially true if your husband was a pastor or deacon in the church. You provided the necessary support in order for him to carry out his responsibilities. At times your home was a hive of activity. Furthermore, many become widows after their children have grown up, left the family home, and perhaps moved away a considerable distance. In the Western world, the day has long since passed when parents and their married children would live around the corner from one another. Sadly, the all-too-frequent breakdown of family relationships complicates matters further. In such circumstances, home can become a very lonely place.

God was well aware of the danger of being isolated and cut off. In Deuteronomy 16:11–14 he gave specific commandments regarding the old-covenant Feast of Weeks and Feast of Tabernacles. Regarding the first, the Lord said, 'You shall rejoice before the LORD your God, you and your son and your daughter, your male servant and your female servant, the Levite who is within your gates, the stranger and the fatherless and the widow who are among you, at the place where the LORD your God chooses to make His name abide. And you shall remember that you were a slave in Egypt, and you shall be careful to observe these statutes' (vv. 11–12). Similar words follow with regard to the second feast: 'You shall observe the Feast of Tabernacles seven days, when you have gathered from your threshing floor and from your winepress. And you shall rejoice in your feast, you and your son and your daughter, your male servant and your female servant and the Levite, the stranger and the fatherless and the widow, who are within your gates' (vv. 13–14).

In the midst of your tears and sense of loneliness you might think that the last thing you want to do is to get up and go and gather with the people of God and rejoice with them. But your heavenly Father is wiser than that and has established an important principle which is followed through in the life of the new-covenant people of God, the church. Here in Deuteronomy God, in effect, says to Israel, 'Make sure that everyone, your widows included, are present when you gather before me to celebrate these feasts.' Everyone in the old-covenant community was to be there in order to recall the goodness of God in the provision of food and another harvest. As a Christian widow, you are still a vital part of the people of God. If you are a widow but not a Christian, here, among Christians, is the place to find out more about God.

The same principle applied in the church. Widows in the church in Jerusalem who were the recipients of daily food also participated in the life and worship of the church (Acts 6:1–7). Similarly, in 1 Timothy 5:3–16, those who were 'really widows' and were on the widows' list (v. 9) had been, and probably still were, active in doing good works (v. 10). It would have been very strange if they were not present at the gatherings for the worship of God. We do not know how old Dorcas was when she died or whether she was a widow herself. A husband and children are not mentioned in Acts 9:36–43, but we do know that she had been 'full of good works and charitable deeds' (v. 36). The widows in the church were the ones who benefited from her ministry (v. 39).

We learn from these and similar passages that widows were not only ministered to but were also active in the worship and life of the church. They were not meant to be ignored or isolated. The loss of your husband will have been not only devastating but also disruptive, ruining the long-established patterns of your life. If your husband suffered a long illness, you may not have been able to attend the meetings of the church as often as you once did because of necessary hospital visits or caring for him in your home. Now you are alone you may be tempted to continue to stay away from church, not least because you anticipate that it will only increase your grief and you will feel very awkward if you suddenly break down in tears. In the long term, you may conclude that, because you cannot do what you once did, there is not much point in continuing to attend. That is contrary to God's will. You need now to be part of the worshipping people of God more than ever. There is joy to be found in such activity because God calls his people together to worship him. He is present with them. You are to enter into that joy. Stay away, and you will only add to your troubles.

The Lord made provision for and issued a command

to Israel to ensure that widows were not left out. It is important to re-establish the normal pattern of attendance as soon as possible. That means being present at the meetings of the church so that your soul is fed and you enjoy fellowship with God and meet your brothers and sisters in Christ. Rejoicing in God, giving thanks to him, singing his praises, and remembering his death in the Lord's Supper are possible in the midst of great sorrow. A great part of your stability—far more than perhaps you will appreciate at first—will be dependent on you taking your place among the people of God as you gather together to worship him.

However, some might say, 'But my circumstances are different! I have children to care for. I cannot possibly get out mid-week, and Sundays will not be easy, and if just one of the children falls ill, that will prevent me from coming.' In such instances your church ought to make some arrangements with you for practical help to be provided so that you can participate as fully as possible in the life of the church.

God never intended any of his people to be cut off and isolated from the worship, life, and ministry of the church of the Lord Jesus Christ. That church is vital to your sanctification, your sanity, and your well-being as a Christian woman. It is in this context that you will learn in your new circumstances to serve Christ and to be served. Even more importantly, it is through the life and ministry of the church that you will find a great measure of relief and healing in the midst of your troubles.

Chapter 7

God's salvation in Zarephath

So she said, 'As the LORD your God lives,
I do not have bread, only a handful of
flour in a bin, and a little oil in a jar; and
see, I am gathering a couple of sticks that
I may go in and prepare it for myself and
my son, that we may eat it, and die.'
1 Kings 17:12

Let us consider another example of God's care for the widow. The plight of the widow of Zarephath was acute. Famine threatened not only Israel but all the surrounding area including Zarephath, which belonged to Sidon. The king of Sidon was Ethbaal, the father of Jezebel. His name meant 'Baal is alive', which was ironic because, as the supposed god of fertility and life, Baal was a total failure. This poor widow and her one son faced starvation and death. Thin and emaciated, she seemed quietly resigned to her lot. Very shortly the famine would account for two more victims—until, that is, Elijah, the prophet of the Lord God of Israel, interrupted the widow's pathetic search for a few sticks for the fire in order to cook their last meal.

Our Lord Jesus Christ knew this account well. In Luke 4:25–26 he recounted that Elijah had not been sent to widows in Israel during the famine but to the widow of Zarephath, a Gentile living under an idolatrous king. Like Ruth before her, she was to experience the blessing of the God of Israel, and to discover that he was the living God and that he alone could deliver her and her son. It is yet another story in the Bible that drives home the point that God cares for the widow and is ready to show his power and his kindness when it is not expected, when she is beyond human help. That is so characteristic of our God!

How did she know about the God of Elijah? We are not told, but 1 Kings 17:12 seems to indicate that she had some knowledge, however vague it might have been. Elijah asked for something that was, on a merely human level, out of the question. He asked her to carry on with her task of collecting sticks, to return home and prepare the food, and then to give him the first helping! Only then would she and her son eat (v. 13). Before giving her that instruction, however, he had urged her not to be afraid. In his next breath Elijah explained why the Lord God of Israel had spoken. Elijah assured her that the bin containing her flour would not be used up, and the jar in which she kept the oil would not run dry until the day the Lord sent rain on the earth once again (v. 14). This lady did everything Elijah told her to do, and the Lord God of Israel did everything he promised that he would do (vv. 15–16). In this way, Elijah was provided for during the famine, and the widow and her son were kept from dying.

God was willing to act in this way for a widow who was not an Israelite. If you are not yet a Christian, you should not be discouraged by thinking that you are excluded. The Lord did not despise this lady for being a widow, nor for being a Gentile. She became the means by which God preserved the life of Elijah, his servant. In so doing, her own life and that of her son were preserved. She was not rich, she was not well known, and we do not even know her name. Nevertheless, God chose to honour this poor, starving lady. God did not simply 'use' her but blessed her in remarkable ways. She was privileged to provide bed and board for God's servant for a period of perhaps two years. She was 'well paid' for her labours by God. By making one small cake for Elijah she was repaid with many more for her son and herself.

Furthermore, she came to know the God of Elijah. She displayed a confidence in God and in his Word. She might have protested to Elijah and told him that she and her son were in a more desperate situation than he was and that therefore they should eat first. Here was a hungry man

who had been on a long journey and who might eat all
the cakes she was about to make! She might have called
into question the promise of God to keep on supplying
the flour and the oil. Instead, this widow responded in
faith and was blessed by God: 'she went away and did
according to the word of Elijah; and she and he and her
household ate for many days. The bin of flour was not
used up, nor did the jar of oil run dry, according to the
word of the LORD which He spoke by Elijah' (vv. 15–16).

This is God's way. You may feel that you are very
insignificant and that there is not much you can do. You
may be in a desperate situation like this widow. Yet the
Lord relieved this widow in her distress and provided for
her in unusual ways during the desperate days of famine.
Do you not think that he is willing and able to draw
alongside you in your troubles? You are a Christian, you
have been purchased with the blood of his Son, the Lord
Jesus Christ, and you are precious in his eyes. Whatever
has happened to you, however your circumstances have
changed, you still belong to him. His love can never be
removed from you. His promises to you in Jesus Christ
have not been withdrawn because you have become
a widow. He stands ready to prove to you in new
circumstances that he is your God.

What if you are not a Christian? Is your case hopeless?
Are you excluded? If there was mercy for the widow of
Zarephath, why should there not be mercy for you? If

there was mercy from God for Ruth, the young widow from Moab, then why not for you? Can he not bring you under the shelter of his own wings? Go to him now and plead the examples of his mercy to Ruth and the widow of Zarephath as reasons why he should hear your cries for mercy and salvation. Come to him, that your faith might rest in the one true and living God and in his Son, Jesus Christ.

The living God of Israel came to the rescue of the widow of Zarephath. Baal had left her to perish because he was no god at all. There are gods like that that we invent; they always fail when we need them most. This widow did exactly as Elijah said. She trusted and obeyed the word of God and staked her life on his promise. She continued to learn to live by faith. I imagine there were days when she had her doubts. Perhaps there were other days when she took God's provision for granted. Her doubts and forgetfulness were rebuked every single day when she went to her kitchen larder. There was the flour bin, together with the jar of oil that she had emptied the day before. They were both full again. God had kept his promise. Each day she learned to be thankful to God, to trust him, and to live on his kindness and powerful provision for her and her son.

Chapter 8

Resurrection in Zarephath

And Elijah took the child and brought him down from the upper room into the house, and gave him to his mother. And Elijah said, 'See, your son lives!'
1 Kings 17:23

The story of God's kindness to the widow of Zarephath did not end with the miraculous supply of food. Having enjoyed his benefits for a time, perhaps the widow imagined that her circumstances would continue unchanged as long as Elijah lodged in her home. She was in for a rude awakening. The miraculous supply of food did not prevent her son from becoming sick and from dying (1 Kings 17:17). She had been through a crisis before, when her husband had died, and another when she and her son faced starvation and death. We are not told how she coped with the first crisis; we have seen how God came to her aid in the second.

This third crisis was more than she could take. Her confidence in God and in his servant Elijah was shattered. In her new affliction she spoke hastily and turned on Elijah. Her tone was one of angry and bitter accusation: 'What have I to do with you, O man of God? Have you come to me to bring my sin to remembrance, and to kill my son?' (v. 18). She reminds us of 'Mrs Mara' in her bitterness. It is hard to be composed and rational when troubles come suddenly and shatter our calm. In her panic and anger she forgot all about the past mercies and the miraculous, daily provision for her needs. Perhaps she even thought that it was pointless God blessing her and her son in that way if now he visited her in judgement because of her sin. Did it not seem as if God was now playing some kind of cruel trick on her, that he indeed had deceived her? If so, he could not be trusted. She resorted to thinking that this was God's punishment for her sin, and put the blame on Elijah for killing her son. Then she made certain that Elijah knew how she felt!

Was she right to blame the man of God? Certainly not, but anyone who has been through a similar crisis can identify with this response to new and sudden sorrows and hardships. You may well have reacted in a similar fashion when the Lord took away your husband. It is right to mourn, and you may have cried every day for weeks, perhaps months. But if the sorrows turn to anger and bitterness and false accusations against God, it can never be right. Such reactions are counterproductive in the long run and cause even more distress. Above all, they drive a wedge between you and God. In a crisis like this the most important thing is to hold on tightly to God, to trust him in the midst of the darkness.

What happened to the widow's son? Elijah did not rebuke the widow but took her son out of her arms and carried him to the upper room that he had made his home during his stay. After laying him on the bed, he cried out to the Lord. Perhaps Elijah was puzzled by the tragedy that had now overtaken the household. He pleaded with God in the light of the great affliction that had now come upon this woman. Stretching himself out on the child three times he prayed, 'O Lord my God, I pray, let this child's soul come back to him' (v. 21). The Scriptures tell us that God heard his voice and the soul of the child came back to him (v. 22). The closing verses of this passage record the joyful reunion as Elijah gave the young boy back to his mother alive and well. Listen to her testimony now: no longer angry and bitter she exclaimed to Elijah, 'Now by this I know that you are a man of God, and that the word of the Lord in your mouth is the truth' (v. 24). Not only was her son restored to life, so, too, was her faith in God.

You may read that happy ending and say that you too

would be able to rejoice as this widow did if the Lord God restored the life of your husband and gave him back to you. Yet I cannot recall one example in the Bible where God brought back to life the husband of a widow. Let us understand that it is not a matter of God's ability but of his wisdom and his will. Suppose the Lord did restore your husband to life. Having gone through the joy of receiving him back, would you really want to go through the loss and the prolonged process of grieving a second time? The day must come when we will all die. For your husband, that day has already come. It is God's will that you accept that he himself has removed your husband. On some days, that is easier to believe than on others. But the Lord has not abandoned you in your loss and he will provide for you for the remainder of your life.

Furthermore, if your husband was a Christian, consider what he has now gained as a result of his death. He is with Christ, 'which is far better' (Phil. 1:23). To die is gain for a Christian, and our Saviour also gains from the death of his saints. It is the beginning of the fulfilment of his own desires and saving work, for he prayed that 'they … may be with Me where I am, that they may behold My glory which You have given me' (John 17:24). You should learn now to be more forward-looking, much more than you were before, filling your mind with what Christ has gained, with what your husband has gained, and with what you yourself will one day gain, rather than backwards to what you have lost.

God raised the widow's son to life. Listening to Elijah's prayer, we sense that he was a man of tenderness. He recognized the widow's affliction and felt it acutely. He spoke to God as the one who had 'brought tragedy on the widow with whom I lodge' (1 Kings 17:20). Yet he pleaded earnestly with God, the God of the widow. He was well acquainted with the Law of Moses and with the merciful heart of God towards widows in their distress and needs. Having lodged with this widow for some months, he knew that once he left her home she would again become vulnerable. Her son was her only means of support and comfort. Furthermore, God's reputation in Sidon was at stake. When Elijah finally left, this widow had a glowing account of all that the living God of Israel had done for her and her son.

That same God is able to meet all of your needs as a widow. He will prove himself to you in many different ways. He will not restore your husband to life at this point in time—that awaits the resurrection. Far greater troubles might come—the earth could be removed and the mountains be carried into the midst of the sea, as Psalm 46 states. Yet that same psalm affirms, 'God is our refuge and strength, a very present help [or "an abundantly available help"] in trouble' (v. 1). Few other psalms breathe the same spirit of confidence in God in the midst of troubles.

That confidence is not for special super-saints, it is for all his children. It is for widows as widows, who have learned and are learning of God's abundantly available help to them in all their distress. Therefore, place all your trust and confidence in him.

Chapter 9

The sympathy and indignation of Christ

Therefore, when Jesus saw her [Mary] weeping, and the Jews who came with her weeping, He groaned in the spirit and was troubled.
John 11:33

The ways in which the prophet Elijah ministered to the widow of Zarephath form a natural link to considering the disposition of the Lord Jesus Christ towards widows during his earthly ministry. Sitting in the temple one day, Jesus was observing how people were putting money into the treasury. There were the rich, putting in large amounts of money, but among the crowd he noticed a solitary widow, literally 'one widow, poor'. Her contribution was two mites, the smallest copper coins in use. Drawing his disciples to himself Jesus gave them an instructive lesson, telling them that this 'one widow, poor' had in fact put more into the treasury than the many rich people. After the widow had given her two mites she had nothing left. By her giving, this widow declared her total trust in God's care for her, being willing to give to God her last means of support. This incident, recorded in Mark 12:41–44, is one of several in the Gospels that tell us how Jesus noticed widows.

The Lord Jesus not only observed this widow, but he also understood her plight. He knew that death had visited her home; he knew her poverty; he knew what it meant for her to give those two remaining mites. There were others, like the widow of Nain, who had suffered the additional loss of her one remaining son (Luke 7:11–17). When Jesus was dying on the cross he displayed great concern for his own widowed mother (John 19:25–27). We will consider these in the following chapters. According to Christ, some rich widows were subjected to financial exploitation by the scribes and the Pharisees (Mark 12:40; Matt. 23:14). Whatever their circumstances, Jesus was thoroughly aware that the death of a husband exposed widows to unusual, even unique, situations of distress.

What is even more significant, however, is to discover that Jesus understood death. He understood how death invaded the life of a widow, robbing her of her closest companion and leaving her destitute, lonely, and vulnerable. It was the result of living in a fallen, sinful world. And he had come into that fallen world, where sin, and the distress caused by sin and death, held sway.

When Lazarus died it does not appear that he left behind a widow but two grieving sisters, Mary and Martha (John 11:1–44). We are informed that Jesus loved each one of them (v. 5), and Lazarus in particular (v. 3). When he came to the tomb of Lazarus, we are told that 'Jesus wept' (v. 35). He did not weep merely because of his love for Lazarus and his sisters; much more was involved. In verse 33 we read that, as Jesus saw Mary and the Jews weeping with her, 'He groaned in the spirit and was troubled'. In order to stress how deeply this situation affected our Lord we are told in verse 38 that on his way to the tomb of Lazarus he was 'again groaning in Himself'. Faced with death, our Lord not only displayed great compassion towards those who experienced the sorrows of death, but he also displayed anger against death. This 'groaning' could be translated as 'being moved with intense indignation'.

What was it that provoked such deeply felt emotions in the Lord? He was reacting to the evil of death. He felt its unnaturalness. Death, as the king of terrors, oppressed men and women. It was an invader that brought misery into the world he had originally created good. Confronted by the evil of death, Jesus was profoundly disturbed in his spirit.

It was not only the evil of death that provoked him to

such anger; Jesus knew that behind death lies the one who has the power of death. Furthermore, it was death and Satan whose powers he had come to destroy. Tears of sympathy filled his eyes, but he was also angry. He came to the tomb of Lazarus ready to do battle with the arch-enemy. He was the one who had come as the Saviour into this fallen world where death reigns, in order to conquer death, Satan, and hell. He proceeded to raise Lazarus from the dead—a decisive declaration of his triumphant power.

Grieving widows can draw much-needed consolation from such a Saviour. No doubt at some point you have been angry because death has taken your loved one from you. It is not wrong to be angry when confronted by the evil of death. If it were wrong, then our Lord would have been guilty of sin. However, if your anger is directed against God and you find yourself beginning to blame him for what has happened, such anger is invariably sinful and it will prevent you from laying hold of the all-conquering Saviour by faith. Now you need to learn to turn from this sinful anger and see the power and compassion of Jesus Christ and entrust yourself to him.

When God's Son made this world, he made it good. Sin, and death, which is the wages of sin, are evil. No cool indifference or unconcern towards death ever existed in the heart of the Redeemer. If you would enjoy true comfort in your heart, grasp this in faith. He came to save us from evil, including the evil of death. He was deeply troubled by the oppressor and now, as the living Saviour, he feels for you deeply, just as he once felt for Mary, for Martha, and for Lazarus. He is not standing far off, aloof and unfeeling, watching you go through pain and sorrow. While on earth he was 'moved with intense indignation'. He acted decisively by raising Lazarus from the dead. Then, driven by compassion and that deep indignation, he secured our redemption through his own death on the cross at Calvary and through his resurrection from the dead. Martha believed these precious words: 'I am the resurrection and the life. He who believes in Me, though he may die, he shall live. And whoever lives and believes in Me shall never die' (vv. 25–26).

This story about Mary, Martha, and Lazarus reveals to us the very heart of our Redeemer, who is the resurrection and the life. Do you believe what he said to Martha? Your husband has died, but if he was a true believer in Christ, he shall live. What is more, if you are a believer, though you too will one day die, you also shall live. Paul speaks of the death of a Christian as being 'absent from the body and … present with the Lord' (2 Cor. 5:8). The grief you now experience is real and distressing but it will not last for ever. And your grief will not end up being intensified by the horrors of hell. Look beyond your grief to the great salvation that Jesus Christ has purchased for you both and avoid dwelling only on what you have lost. Go to Jesus confidently, knowing how he reacted to death, knowing that he has triumphed over death. He is no stranger to tears, for he wept at the tomb of Lazarus. All these things are intended to draw you to the Saviour each time the floodgates of grief open and threaten to drown you. You will find, as did Martha, Mary, and Lazarus, that he will never fail you. He is able to bring unspeakable comfort to your soul.

Perhaps you are reading this and you are not a believer in Christ, and you are repeatedly overcome by a very real sense of helplessness in the face of death. You may have been angered by your helplessness and by all that you have gone through. Do not despair, and do not let your despair drive you away from this Redeemer. You have sinned, you have not kept God's law, you have not been thankful to him. You may have lived your life with hardly any thought of God. Perhaps you are thinking that these things must surely disqualify you. On the contrary, they are all the more reason to go to Jesus Christ. Go to him with your sins. Confess them to him and turn away from them. Go in your despair and cry out to him for mercy and salvation. Pour out your heart to him, and tell him how sinful and helpless you are. Take the words he spoke to grieving Martha in verses 25–26 and then, like her, place your faith in the Son of God—the Redeemer, Jesus Christ. He is the Saviour of sinners. He is willing and able to save you from death and from your sins that are the cause of death.

Chapter 10

Resurrection in Nain

*And when He came near the gate of the city,
behold, a dead man was being carried out, the
only son of his mother; and she was a widow
… When the Lord saw her, He had compassion
on her and said to her, 'Do not weep.'*
Luke 7:12–13

In the Gospels we read of three people whom Jesus raised from the dead: Lazarus; the daughter of Jairus, the synagogue ruler; and the son of the widow of Nain. The last of these events is recorded in Luke 7:11–17. We are not told how long this lady had been a widow. Like Naomi, her situation was tragic. When we are old we expect to die, but how sad it is when a parent faces the death of a son or a daughter cut down in the prime of life. The situation reminds us of that of the widow of Zarephath, which we looked at earlier. The dead man we read of in Luke was the only son of his mother. With his death her one remaining source of protection and financial support had been snatched away from her. Any hope of perpetuating the family line had also been vanquished. She had already been through one trial with the death of her husband, and had possibly had to raise her son without his help and influence. Now a second tragedy struck her and her tears knew no bounds.

Jesus met the sombre funeral procession coming out of Nain as he, together with many disciples and a large crowd, entered the city. Imagine the scene. He was probably at the head of his group. They would have seen and heard the weeping of another large crowd coming towards them, with hired mourners and musicians. At the head of this crowd were a few men carrying the covered body of a man, followed closely by a grieving mother— this widow. The eyes of Jesus fixed on her. His heart went out to her in her specific need at that very moment. He knew the reasons for her tears. Having taken account of all that was happening to this widow, he immediately had compassion on her. He spoke a kind word of command and told her to stop weeping.

Jesus was full of compassion. When he showed compassion, not only did he feel inwardly a response of pity and mercy, but also his heart went out in acts of kindness. The mercy he showed was divine mercy. The entire life of our Lord was a mission of mercy. Peter summarized that mission by declaring how 'God anointed

Jesus of Nazareth with the Holy Spirit and with power, who went about going good ... for God was with Him' (Acts 10:38). This event in Luke is therefore one of the many occasions when we see this goodness of God in full display.

In some cases, those in need cried out to the Lord for mercy, like the two blind men on the outskirts of Jericho. He had compassion on them and touched their eyes, and they received their sight (Matt. 20:29–34). On this occasion at Nain he received no request for help; all he heard were the cries of weeping. The sight and sounds of that widow's distress were enough to set the heart of Jesus throbbing with compassion. Perhaps in your sorrows you have found yourself barely able to utter any words in prayer. The measure of compassion the Lord Jesus displays is never in accordance with the strength of your prayers and cries. It is true that he hears the weakest cries, but he even shows compassion when there are no cries for help. He sees an individual in distress and the very sight is enough to draw out pity from his heart.

In the Lord's dealings with this widow and her son we see the love of Jesus for her in particular. She and her son were helpless in the face of sin and the misery that it brings. Christ came to their aid. Without any request from anyone he came and touched the open coffin, stopping the procession. He spoke to the dead man, 'Young man, I say to you, arise.' Once more his pity was joined with his power. The young man sat up and began to speak. The tenderness of the Lord Jesus was captured by Luke when he wrote, 'And He presented him to his mother' (v. 15). That tells us that Jesus knew exactly what raising the man from the dead would mean for her. She would not have to face old age alone. Her son would be the staff and stay of her remaining years.

As a widow, whatever your precise circumstances may be, you are the object of Christ's tender love, compassion, and power. Here is the one who was able to remove the cause of the widow's tears. When he raised this young man from the dead, the crowds who saw the miracle glorified God. They said that he had to be a great prophet, and that God had visited his people (v. 16).

What Jesus did for the widowed mother and her son he will one day do for all those who die in Christ. When Christians die, they are present with the Lord. They are waiting for the resurrection, 'for the adoption, the redemption of [their] body' (Rom. 8:23). He will bring complete salvation when he raises all his people from the dead incorruptible. He will certainly reunite us with all our loved ones who have died in him. We are not to sorrow, then, as those who have no hope, 'For if we believe that Jesus died and rose again, even so God will bring with Him those who sleep in Jesus' (1 Thes. 4:14). Here is the only firm foundation for true comfort.

Chapter 11

The love of Jesus for his mother

When Jesus therefore saw His mother, and the disciple whom He loved standing by, He said to His mother, 'Woman, behold your son!' Then He said to the disciple, 'Behold your mother!' And from that hour that disciple took her to his own home.
John 19:26–27

One of the remarkable things about the sufferings and crucifixion of the Saviour was that, despite all his agonies, he remained selfless and occupied himself with the various needs of different people. Before his betrayal and arrest he had prayed not only for himself but also for his disciples and for all who would believe on him (John 17). He had also prayed very specifically for Peter, that his faith would not fail in his coming temptation (Luke 22:31–34). While he was tried by the Sanhedrin the Lord Jesus knew what was going on in the courtyard outside as Peter denied him three times.

While others were filled with sorrow as they saw Jesus being led away to be crucified, he himself visualized the impending judgement and told the daughters of Jerusalem not to weep for him but for themselves and their children (Luke 23:28). Even as he was being crucified he showed mercy to the penitent thief alongside him. The thief was forgiven and entered with Christ into paradise (Luke 23:43). Those events are well known by many, but the tender regard that Jesus displayed for his mother is often overlooked.

We find that John, who recorded this tender regard, was the very disciple who received the sacred charge from the Lord Jesus and assumed responsibility for Mary, the mother of Jesus. Many years before, when Mary had visited her cousin Elizabeth, she had heard her repeat the words of the angel Gabriel: 'Blessed are you among women!' (Luke 1:42, 28). At this point Mary was already carrying Jesus in her womb. That joy and privilege had then been tempered by Simeon following the birth of Jesus: 'Behold, this Child is destined for the fall and rising of many in Israel, and for a sign which will be spoken against (yes, a sword will pierce through your own soul also), that the thoughts of many hearts may be revealed' (Luke 2:34–35). Some might think that Simeon was being a pessimist. On the contrary, he was being realistic. God gave him the difficult and delicate task of warning the mother of the Lord Jesus that preceding the redemption of God's people there would be bitter sorrow and anguish for Israel, for her son, and for herself.

When she first heard of the sword that would pierce her own motherly heart she would not have fully understood what that meant. When, thirty years or so later, she stood at the cross and saw the suffering of her son, she felt the pain of that sword-thrust piercing into the depths of her womanhood. 'The heart knows its own bitterness, and a stranger does not share its joy' (Prov. 14:10). No human being can make someone else fully understand exactly how he or she feels in a time of bitter sorrow or exceeding joy. However, Jesus entered into the sorrows of his mother as he hung on the cross. His own pain and sorrows did not cut him off from the needs of others. They did not deaden his deep feelings and sympathy as he discerned the internal wounds caused by the sword that was at that very moment being plunged into the heart of his own mother.

At this point in her life Mary was almost certainly widowed. Jesus would not have commended Mary to John's care if there had been a husband or family in a position to care and provide for her. But now, with strong filial love and great tenderness, he obeyed his own commandments, in particular the fifth commandment, by committing his mother to the care of John and pressing on John a sacred obligation to provide for her. John's response was immediate. We read that 'from that hour that disciple took her to his own home' (John 19:27).

Here is a Saviour of matchless tenderness, sympathy, and understanding. He did not leave Mary silver, gold, or precious possessions; they might have been a means of providing some relief. Rather, he bestowed on her something far more valuable—a secure home for her, together with the love, the care, and the provision of the man who was recognized as being closest to Jesus and the most loving and tender-hearted of the disciples. On that day John undertook to provide for her well-being for the rest of her life. He was the provision Jesus made for his mother.

The Lord Jesus never forgets anyone who loves him, even in that person's deepest distress. According to Mark 3:34–35, he regarded anyone who did the will of God as his brother, his sister, and his mother. All such people are his family members. Some of your friends may be unsure whether they should talk to you about your husband for fear of adding to your sorrows. That tends to add to your isolation. On the other hand, they may not be very good listeners. You long for someone who will listen to you and understand you as you unburden your sorrows and distress. That someone is your Saviour. The love of the Lord Jesus has no length or breadth that we can measure, and you should therefore pour out your heart to him assured of that love, knowing that he understands and will never fail you. His mother knew that, and it was affirmed by his provision for her in the midst of his terrible sufferings.

At the same time we learn that Jesus Christ made human provision for his mother. In later chapters we will consider that provision which Christ makes for widows through the extended family and his church. This should not surprise us, as the Lord is only fulfilling and applying his Word written in the Old Testament Scriptures.

Chapter 12

Omnipotent compassion

Seeing then that we have a great High Priest who has passed through the heavens, Jesus the Son of God, let us hold fast our confession. For we do not have a High Priest who cannot sympathize with our weaknesses, but was in all points tempted as we are, yet without sin.
Hebrews 4:14–15

Real sympathy for widows is a comparatively rare thing in this world. Samuel Rutherford learnt to be a compassionate and faithful pastor to some of Christ's suffering saints. He himself experienced the deaths of his two children in their infancy, followed by that of his young wife, Eupham, after a long illness.[1] Rutherford felt desolated, weary, and lonely. Yet out of his sorrows he learnt to lead others to the sympathizing great High Priest, the Lord Jesus Christ, and impart to them some of the comforts he had received from him.

Sadly, instead of sympathy, exploitation or neglect are

far too commonly experienced by widows. For example, in Mark 12:38–40 the Lord Jesus warned his disciples against the conduct of the scribes. Some of them made it their practice to target rich widows. Scribes probably functioned as consultants in estate planning for these rich widows. Such a situation gave them opportunity to persuade vulnerable widows that they should use their money for holy purposes. They could either give it to the temple or to the scribe for his holy work. Either way, there was the very real possibility of personal gain for the scribe. In verses 41–44 Mark appears to draw a contrast, not only between those who gave out of their abundance and the widow who gave out of her poverty, but also between the greed and spiritual poverty of the scribes in verse 40 and the giving and the spiritual wealth of the widow in verse 44. On the one hand, the scribe extracted all he could from the widow, while on the other hand, the widow put in all she had, 'her whole livelihood', when she put her two mites into the temple treasury.

This warning, together with the woe pronounced by Christ against the scribes and Pharisees for their greed (Matt. 23:14), reminds us of the ways in which the Old Testament prophets spoke out in God's name against those who were ready to exploit the widow.[2]

The Lord Jesus Christ always upheld and fulfilled the Law of God. He was the living embodiment of his own law. We would therefore expect him to uphold all the laws and commandments regarding widows and display understanding, sympathy, and concern for widows, defending them against those who would abuse them. This is what we find in Mark 12:40–44. The same truth lies behind the parable of the persistent widow in Luke 18:1–8. As we noted earlier, this poor widow was suffering a double injustice. On the one hand, someone was treating her unjustly and she asked the judge to act for her. He, on the other hand, ignored her but then decided to obtain justice for her because he did not want her to keep pestering him. The lesson of this parable concerns persistence in prayer. God is far more willing to hear us than the unjust judge was to hear the widow, and he will certainly avenge his elect who cry to him day and night. Jesus would not have used the example of the widow if it did not reflect the kind of injustice to which widows were subjected in his day.

Furthermore, if God is revealed in the Old Testament as 'A father of the fatherless, a defender of widows' (Ps. 68:5), this is also true of the Lord Jesus Christ. He is none other than God in the flesh. The widow, the one bereaved, is, as we have seen, the special object of Christ's concern. That is a further reason why we find him denouncing the exploitation of the widow and showing love and compassion towards her. Everything we discovered about God's attitude to the widow in the Old Testament Scriptures is true of Jesus Christ. It is not simply a matter of Jesus Christ obeying the Old Testament laws; he is like his Father, for he is the embodiment of his Father's love. And that is precisely what we see in the Gospels. So when, for example, Jesus saw the widow of Nain leading a procession to bury her son, he was moved to compassion (Luke 7:13). It was divine compassion displayed by the incarnate Son.

Is Jesus Christ willing to show today the same kind of compassion that he showed to the widows during his earthly ministry? Hebrews 4:14–16 speaks clearly of our compassionate and great High Priest. He is none other than Jesus, the Son of God, who has now passed through the heavens. That means he has entered once for all into the heavenly sanctuary, there to appear on behalf of all his people. He is there as our Mediator and our Redeemer, for he is truly man and truly God. Thus we have his pity joined with his power, what someone once called 'omnipotent compassion'.

In verse 15 the writer to the Hebrews is emphasizing this sympathy, the compassion of our Redeemer. That sympathy is connected with our weaknesses, particularly with our overcoming temptations (or testings), in order that we might not give up but rather learn to persevere. Our Lord Jesus Christ was tested throughout his life. Recall Satan's temptations in the wilderness when Christ was tempted by feelings of self-concern, then by the enticements of popular acclaim and ambition for power.

In Gethsemane he wrestled with the temptation to draw back from the terrifying ordeal of the cross. While hanging on the cross he was taunted by the crowds, 'If You are the Son of God, come down from the cross' (Matt. 27:40).

What has this to do with you as a widow? Is not your experience a testing, a situation in which the devil will tempt you to despair of God, to make you think that God has abandoned you, or to have you wallow in self-pity? In the devil's hand, widowhood easily becomes an opportunity for sin, and that is precisely the malicious intent of your enemy. In the hand of God, however, such testing becomes an experience in which you learn to prove the 'omnipotent compassion' of your great High Priest. You know grief and loneliness, but did anyone experience grief and loneliness like the Lord Jesus Christ? Isaiah tells us that he was 'despised and rejected by men, a Man of sorrows and acquainted with grief' (Isa. 53:3). He also knew what it was like to be isolated. He was betrayed by Judas, deserted by all the disciples, and denied by Peter. Alone, he stood before the Sanhedrin, then before Pilate, where he was mocked by the soldiers, before he finally cried out on the cross, 'My God, My God, why have You forsaken Me?' (Mark 15:34). He persevered through those trials and temptations. He was tempted in all points as we are, yet was without sin.

This same Lord Jesus is in heaven as our great High Priest and he is able to enter fully into the sorrows, loneliness, and the temptations that widowhood brings. We are exhorted to come boldly to the throne of grace (Heb. 4:16) in order to 'obtain mercy and find grace to help in time of need'. The temptation will be to draw back instead of drawing near to God. Satan will remind you of your sins and failings, and of your anger and despair, tempting you to think that God has abandoned you and suggesting that there is no point in your coming. The difficulty of the struggle should be an encouragement to come boldly through Jesus Christ. See what you are promised: mercy and grace. That is the very help you need—help that is appropriate to the particular needs of the moment. There are no grounds for despair because of the 'omnipotent compassion' of Christ.

Chapter 13

Deacons and the care of widows

Now in those days, when the number of the disciples was multiplying, there arose a complaint against the Hebrews by the Hellenists, because their widows were neglected in the daily distribution ... 'Therefore, brethren, seek out from among you seven men of good reputation, full of the Holy Spirit and wisdom, whom we may appoint over this business.'
Acts 6:1, 3

As the church in Jerusalem continued to grow it faced a number of problems. One of them related to the serving of tables (v. 2), and in particular, the care of widows. From the very beginning of the New Testament church the particular needs of widows were met by the church's ministry of mercy. A widow should expect to receive not only spiritual counsel and comfort but also practical help from the church. The provision for needy widows already had a high priority on this church's agenda.

It would seem that, in Acts 6, cultural and social

tensions had come to the fore between the 'purer' Jewish element in the church that spoke Aramaic and were deeply immersed in Jewish culture, and the Grecian Jews, who had adopted the Greek language and culture as their own. The Greek-speaking Jews began to murmur among themselves and perhaps even filed some kind of complaint against the Aramaic-speaking group. 'Our widows are being overlooked,' they were suggesting; 'Hebrew widows are receiving preferential treatment.' They were pointing out that the daily distribution of food was not being carried out in a fair way.

In the first place, we note that this preferential treatment was probably not deliberate. Luke gives no indication that it was the result of partiality. The problem that arose may simply have exposed the shortcomings of the system that was then in use. If the apostles were responsible for the task, it was becoming too much for them. However, if the matter got out of hand it would have caused a serious division in the church in Jerusalem.

Secondly, we observe that, under the leadership of the apostles, the church appointed deacons to resolve this problem. The apostles were persuaded that for them to continue caring for these widows would distract them from their priorities, namely, prayer and the ministry of the Word (v. 4). I believe that the seven men chosen were deacons, appointed by the apostles and the church to reflect the compassion of Christ. In the Old Testament we discovered that God has undertaken to defend and relieve widows. The church in Jerusalem was not creating something new; the members were continuing Old Testament principles and practice.

In the West today the care of widows is largely seen to be the duty of the state. That is not the biblical perspective. I often reflect on whether our churches today have deacons who see themselves as true ministers of mercy, called to show the compassion of Christ. Do they see the ongoing care of widows as a priority among their other concerns and therefore as a permanent item on their agenda? Many widows, I fear, are too easily forgotten and simply left to do the best they can once the funeral is over. Who is going to speak up on their behalf?

There is one further important observation to make. It was not the creation of the diaconate that led to the care of widows in the church in Jerusalem; the care of widows was firmly in place from the very beginning of that church. The seven spiritually qualified men were appointed to ensure that the task was carried out fully and fairly. What the Scriptures underline is that God's people are to show his mercy, and that the widow's needs are to be supplied by them. The widow has a God-given right to expect the church to visit her in her troubles, to relieve her, and to comfort her.

We can trace the development of that practice in the church in Jerusalem. We discover in Acts 2:44–45 and

4:34–37 that the resources of the church were being pooled on a voluntary basis. Many in the church suffered from poverty. Among those who were most in need were widows. Wealthier individuals, like Barnabas, were selling land and bringing the money to the apostles for use in the church. Both passages inform us that *no one was in need* because the church was providing for everyone. Therefore we conclude that the daily distribution of food was being made out of these voluntary contributions.

Later on, when famine threatened the Judean churches (Acts 11:27–30), the church in Antioch sent relief to the brethren in Jerusalem and Judea. That relief, provided once again on a voluntary basis, was sent to the elders by the hands of Barnabas and Paul. These were trusted men who could be relied upon to ensure that the aid arrived safely in Judea. It is reasonable to suppose that Paul had additional reasons for relieving the needy in Judea. By his opposition to and persecution of the churches prior to his conversion to Christ he had probably been personally responsible for creating widows and orphans by his determination to extinguish this new sect (Acts 8:3; 9:1–2). The care of such widows would therefore have been close to the heart of the apostle.

The Lord Jesus had entrusted his mother to the care of John. Now we see that the care of widows was also entrusted to the church of Christ, and, in particular, to the deacons. Therefore, the widow is not to be left to fend for herself. The relief provided is more than just the teaching ministry of the church. It includes relieving *all* the needs of the widow.

If you are a widow, a Christian, and a member of a church, then you ought never to feel completely alone and abandoned, despite the loss of your husband. If you are not a Christian it might well be that your first taste of God's mercy is experienced in the listening ear of a Christian lady who has also become a widow. It is in the church that the compassion of Christ is to be experienced, not only as it is expressed by the pastors and deacons, but also by the warm and sincere love and concern of each and every member of the body of Christ.

Acts 9:36–41 is a further indication of the ministry of the church to widows. We mention again the lady called Dorcas who was 'full of good works and charitable deeds' (v. 36). It was the widows in particular who were so upset when Dorcas died. She was evidently a talented seamstress, making tunics and garments for these widows (v. 39). Peter raised her from the dead! He called the saints *and* the widows together and presented Dorcas alive. Here was a second resurrection from the dead that was intended to provide specific relief for widows (see Luke 7:11–17).

As a widow going through the process of grieving, you will need to begin to build a new life and cultivate new relationships. Much of the help, comfort, and relief you need will be found among the members of the church of Christ. That is the environment God provides for the growth, well-being, and perseverance of all his people. We also see that the Scriptures are consistent. We have already shown that the worship, the life, and the ministry of the church are an integral part of God's will for you as a widow. What happened in Jerusalem in Acts 6:1–7 underlines this and demonstrates how God's commandments are worked out in practice.

Chapter 14

'Really widows'

Honor widows who are really widows. But if any widow has children or grandchildren, let them first learn to show piety at home and to repay their parents; for this is good and acceptable before God. … But if anyone does not provide for his own, and especially for those of his own household, he has denied the faith and is worse than an unbeliever.
1 Timothy 5:3–4, 8

We have just seen that the Bible stresses the responsibility of the church to care for widows. Does that mean a widow is entitled, then, to assume that the church will provide everything for her because her husband has died? In 1 Timothy 5:3–16 we are provided with clear teaching. The church of Christ is called on to exercise discernment by assessing the particular situation of each widow. There are some widows 'who are really widows'. These we shall consider in a moment. On the other hand, the apostle Paul says that there are other widows who are to be provided for by their families.

All widows need the spiritual comfort of the church's ministry and the warmth of true fellowship, but not all widows have the same circumstances. They may not all need the financial support of the church in order to live. God provides for them through the extended family. To take care of the widow is a matter of Christian obedience for children and for grandchildren (v. 4).

If you are a widow with grown-up children, your children owe you a debt. In God's eyes, caring for a mother who is now in need is a small return for the fifteen to twenty years during which she looked after her children. God requires it: it is good and acceptable to him (v. 4). It may be that for some reason it is not possible for those children to care for their mother. That is something for the church to discern and then to act upon accordingly. It may be, of course, that the children have grown up and not become Christians and refuse to take care of their widowed mother.

Sometimes in this fallen world we do see extreme hard-heartedness. A few years ago there was a spate of what the media in the USA called 'granny-dumping'. Elderly and sometimes sick mothers were just left at hospitals for others to do the caring. Sadly, on one or two occasions I have come across similar situations in the UK when I have discovered that the lonely old lady I have been visiting in a local care home has family near at hand. However, the family rarely if ever come to visit her, show very little love or concern, and never ensure that she is being looked after properly. We live in a world where sin and selfishness have taken deep root in human hearts, sadly leading to hardness of heart and the neglect of parents. Paul says that such attitudes are unthinkable for a Christian—to live like this is to deny the faith, showing oneself worse than an unbeliever (v. 8). Not all unbelievers fail to fulfil their responsibilities to their widowed mothers.

Clearly, some families in Ephesus (where Timothy, the recipient of Paul's letter, was ministering at the time) were falling short of their God-given responsibilities. They were not making any plans to provide for a widowed mother should the need arise (v. 8). Did they not feel any obligation? Were their consciences not stirred? Paul did not mince his words. To deny the faith in this context is to deny by your actions the true Christian compassion and love which are the supreme expressions of true godliness. Such compassion and love are God-like, they are Christ-like. Remember the example of our Lord Jesus Christ. He ensured that his mother was cared for by John even in the hour of his greatest agonies.

What, then, of the ladies who are described in verse 3 as 'really widows'? They were godly, believing ladies who were very vulnerable and needy in that they had no family members to provide for them and were without any means of support. Such a widow really was alone and thus worthy of the church's care and support.

Furthermore, their godliness is described in verse 5: they trusted in God, in particular as the defender of widows. Do you have that trust in God as the defender of widows? Is your confidence in God complemented by a devotion to God expressed in constant supplications and prayers? Here is the widow who enjoys fellowship with God. Anna is a good biblical example of such a lady (Luke 2:36–37). Once she was widowed it appears that she decided not to remarry but devoted herself to the service of the Lord. In this regard she was similar to the unmarried woman in 1 Corinthians 7:34 who was in a position to serve God without being distracted by concerns about pleasing her husband.

The Lord required the church to exercise discernment in providing care and support for the widows among them. The reputations of the church and of the Lord Jesus were at stake. Any widow who devoted herself to pleasure, giving very little care and attention to godliness, would be rejected (1 Tim. 5:6). Paul commanded that only godly widows were to be honoured; that is, they alone were to be supported and to be shown great respect by the church. The word 'honour' has the idea of meeting particular needs, including financial needs. The application is plain. If you are a widow without means or with very limited means, do not proudly refuse the help the church is willing and able to give. This is God's way of taking care of you. On the other hand, if you have financial resources left to you by your husband, or you have believing family members who are in a position to provide for you, do not expect to live off the church.

That does not mean that you have nothing to do with the church regarding financial matters. It could well be that you would benefit from financial advice, whether you are a 'real widow' or not. You would be wise to seek and to receive such advice. It may begin with very practical matters, like paying the bills and getting advice about how to ensure you live within your means. If your husband took care of all those matters you will now have to assume responsibility for your financial affairs. To some it can present a fearful prospect because it is something they do not know much about. Again, do not be so proud as to refuse help and then run the risk of falling into debt because of that refusal. The church should be able to provide someone from its own number or recommend somebody who can help you by explaining the financial implications of becoming a widow, showing you how to adapt to your new financial situation. None of that will be easy, especially in the early months when you are living with the daily experience of grief; that is why you need help.

Here we discover that the Scriptures lay constraints on all parties involved in such situations: the widows, the families who have widows among them, and the church. No one is free to do as he or she pleases. God already has a blue-print in place. In particular, widows are called to be godly, and it is to this subject that we turn in the next chapter.

Chapter 15

Serving Christ as a widow

Do not let a widow under sixty years old be taken into the number, and not unless she has been the wife of one man, well reported for good works: if she has brought up children, if she has lodged strangers, if she has washed the saints' feet, if she has relieved the afflicted, if she has diligently followed every good work.
1 Timothy 5:9–10

Opinions are divided over the precise meaning of these two verses. Some take them to set out the high standard required for—and describe the kind of work to be carried out by—widows who serve in the church. The church, then, has a body of qualified widows who are listed as recognized women workers. Others take the verses to further describe the widows who are 'real widows' (v. 3) and thus worthy of the church's full support. This is not the place to consider the various arguments.

Instead we shall focus on what I believe is a valid application of the passage under consideration. Titus

2:3–5 gives instruction about the role of older women in the church, widows or not. Paul commands Titus in verse 1 of that chapter, 'But as for you, speak the things which are proper for sound doctrine.' Having spoken about the behaviour of the older men he turns to the older women and commands 'the older women likewise, that they be reverent in behavior, not slanderers, not given to much wine, teachers of good things—that they admonish the young women to love their husbands, to love their children, to be discreet, chaste, homemakers, good, obedient to their own husbands, that the word of God may not be blasphemed.'

If we combine what is said here in Titus with 1 Timothy 5:9–10, we have a possible outline for what an older godly widow might set out to accomplish in the remainder of her active life. You will need to build a new life, and if you remain unmarried you may find you have new opportunities to abound in good works. Your own husband has gone, your children are grown up, and you thus have the opportunity to give yourself to serving the Lord and his church. If you have lived a godly life you should possess the maturity, reputation, character, experience, and compassion to serve the Lord and the church. Even if you were converted to Christ in later years and do not possess that same experience and godly maturity, there is still work for you to do, perhaps in tandem with a more experienced Christian.

Being a widow provides you with scope to be a free woman for Christ. Paul does not make it a command when he says to the unmarried and widows, 'It is good for them if they remain even as I am' (1 Cor. 7:8). You are free to remarry, but at the same time you also have the opportunity to serve the Lord without distraction for the rest of your life (1 Cor. 7:34–35). You will need to weigh this carefully before God before you reach a decision. After the death of your husband you will need time to find your feet and readjust. Instead of turning in on yourself, learn to see that becoming a widow may provide you with new opportunities to serve your Lord. If Dorcas was a wealthy widow, she was one who devoted herself to a Christ-like care of others. Look at all the experience you have to pass on, all the lessons you have learned, for example, in those 'hidden years' when you bore the responsibility of bringing up your children while your husband was at work. You might look back and say it was pretty mundane—cooking, cleaning, and caring for the children as they grew up. However, some of those lessons learned are the very things that the next generation of younger parents needs to hear from you.

For example, do you remember those times when you were tempted to ignore sinful behaviour in your children? Those young mothers are facing the same temptations. Or do you remember grappling with those fears that perhaps you and your husband were being too hard on your children, and that if you actually did what the Word of God said regarding verbal reproof and physical punishment, you would turn your children away from you and from God? Today's mothers face even more pressure to think that way, given the current climate of opinion on bringing up children. Have you no advice and instruction to give them? Would you turn a deaf ear to the stressed and frustrated Christian wife and mother who begins to criticize her husband to her friends because she thinks he is lazy and not fulfilling his responsibilities? Or will you seek to draw alongside her and gently but firmly rebuke her, convince her that such conduct is unbecoming of a Christian wife, and show her how she can love her husband and work towards resolving the tension between them?

Is encouragement only the province of men like Barnabas? What about Phoebe, 'a helper of many and of myself also', and the rest of the noble women mentioned together with faithful men in Romans 16:1–16? Consider that a few words of sincere encouragement from you will go a very long way. There are also many practical ways in which you can help. A busy mother with demanding young children sometimes does not have time to bake a tasty cake. Perhaps you have some computer skills which could be put to good use in the church. What about your own peers who are sick in hospital or need a helping hand in the home? Do not leave all the work of reading the

Scriptures, giving encouragement, comforting the weak, and praying with the needy saints to the pastor!

No one is asking you to stand up and speak publicly. Much more valuable is the personal ministry of continued good works and of bringing the Word of Truth to bear in love with wise counsel and much prayer. When Dorcas died the widows in Joppa missed her greatly. When you finally end your life and go to be with Christ, will people miss you and the ministry you exercised while you had the opportunity?

Chapter 16

Younger widows

Therefore I desire that the younger widows marry, bear children, manage the house, give no opportunity to the adversary to speak reproachfully.
1 Timothy 5:14

Should you remarry at some point in the future? The Scriptures are clear: death annuls the marriage relationship. Therefore, there is no sin of immorality involved in remarriage. Once a husband dies the woman is free to remarry (Rom. 7:2–3). At the same time, there is no absolute requirement to remarry. However, if a Christian does remarry, it must be 'in the Lord', as 1 Corinthians 7:39 makes clear (see also 2 Cor. 6:14).

Nevertheless, there are some widows who remain unmarried. Some, like Anna (Luke 2:36–37), have decided to use their circumstances as an opportunity to serve the Lord. Over the years I have been privileged to visit widows who have remained unmarried and in their latter years have been confined to their homes because of ill-health and lack of mobility. Unashamedly they have given themselves to prayer and the reading of the Scriptures. At the time of writing I miss going to see a widow who is now present with her Lord. It is over two years since she died. She was well into her nineties. Why do I miss her? I went to minister to her in the spirit of James 1:27 but invariably came away having been ministered to by her, because of her constant love for and sheer delight in Jesus, her Saviour.

There are other older widows who remain unmarried because they feel that they have no need to remarry or consider that they are now too old, and even some who mistakenly consider remarriage a matter of unfaithfulness to their late husbands. Others decide to remain alone because they are not able to find men whom they judge would make suitable companions.

Becoming a widow can be a time of real temptation. The Bible is always realistic. Those temptations are not unlike those facing single women. One older lady I knew was for many years a faithful member of her church together with her husband. Some months after he died she moved into the home of another man. He was not a Christian and seemed to be more interested in her money than in her. Despite the intervention of the church, its warnings, and its rebukes, she continued unrepentant in this relationship. The church had little option but to exclude her from its membership, although the members remained in contact with her as she still desired, and continued, to attend the church services. Perhaps this lady was desperate and panicked. She certainly did not seek wise counsel. She was led into temptation and sin and made a wrong moral choice. She ought to have trusted God and learned to wait on him, asking him to provide a godly companion as a husband. If you decide to remarry it is very important not to make a rash move and marry the wrong person, only to spend the rest of your life in misery.

So far, we have mentioned only older widows. What about the young? You may be one who now finds herself widowed, for example, as a consequence of your husband having been killed in active service in the armed forces, as the result of a road traffic accident, or from a disease such as cancer. In some cases there may be young children who now have no father and are dependent on a mother who is going to struggle to bring them up on her own. Initially, family and friends can provide support, but that is not a long-term solution. The biblical answer is usually remarriage, for your own sake and for the sake of the children.

Paul is realistic in his words about remarriage. He is aware of the temptations that face widows, especially young widows. He addresses the issues in 1 Timothy 5:11–15. He gives no counsel in this passage to older widows about remarriage. Younger widows are different, however, and his instruction is clear: They should seek to remarry in due course and the church has a responsibility to encourage them in that direction. Until they remarry they may need the help of the church but they should not be put on any list of widows. The apostle gives two reasons. Firstly, in verses 11–12 he says that if they are added to the list and then remarry, they will break their pledge to serve Christ as widows. If any young widow on the list decides to remarry, it will mean that she will then be breaking her vow to serve only the Lord. It would appear that Paul is anxious that a young widow does not make a hasty vow while she is emotionally distraught following the death of her husband, only to find that she has had a change of mind. To break such a vow has serious consequences for her because it will mean that she has abandoned her original commitment to Christ.[1]

Then, secondly, in verses 13–15 he says that if they are cared for by the church, some of them might be tempted to abuse that care. Instead of being godly they could become busybodies and idle gossips, and so be a liability and disgrace to the church of Christ. Others might fall into sexual immorality (vv. 14b–15).

Paul's counsel, then, is plain. He strongly encourages the younger widows to remarry. Let them enter fully into family life (v. 14) and thus eliminate the particular temptations to which they may be exposed. Does this contradict what Paul writes in 1 Corinthians 7:32–40, where he commends remaining single? In that passage Paul commends singleness because in that state a person is able to serve the Lord with undivided attention (v. 34). In verse 39 he says that a widow 'is at liberty to be married to whom she wishes, only in the Lord'.

As a widow you have to work this matter out before God and be convinced in your own mind that it is right for you to remarry. On the one hand, you could consider whether you can follow Anna's example and remain single. The apostle is refreshingly frank in 1 Corinthians 7:8–9. To the unmarried and widows he counsels, 'It is good for them if they remain even as I am; but if they cannot exercise self-control, let them marry. For it is better to marry than to burn with passion.' There is no reason to be ashamed of those sexual desires. They are God-given. Seek to remarry. Remarriage is not only a possibility in the New Testament but is encouraged under the right circumstances. How long should you wait before you remarry? That will depend on individual circumstances, but remarriage to the right person will bring comfort and a renewed sense of security. It is one of the means God provides towards helping you to overcome the grief you still experience.

If you were widowed after only a few years of marriage

it would, I think, be unusual to conclude that you should now remain single. If there are fatherless children involved, then without hesitation you should consider remarriage at the appropriate time. On the other hand, an older woman might well conclude that she can happily remain as a widow without compromising her godliness. Remember that the young Ruth remarried; Naomi, her mother-in-law, and much older than Ruth, remained a widow.

Chapter 17

Standing fast

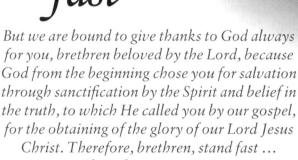

*But we are bound to give thanks to God always
for you, brethren beloved by the Lord, because
God from the beginning chose you for salvation
through sanctification by the Spirit and belief in
the truth, to which He called you by our gospel,
for the obtaining of the glory of our Lord Jesus
Christ. Therefore, brethren, stand fast ...*
2 Thessalonians 2:13–15a

The providential care of God covers every single
circumstance of our lives, including bereavement.
The death of a loved one brings a severe trial to our faith,
and you may well question the truth of God's providence
many times in the process of grieving. Godly submission
is not always easy. However, submitting to God and
realizing that what you are going through is a divinely
ordained trial intended to prove God's faithfulness and
all-sufficiency as your defender, and to test your own
faith, will take you a long way towards accepting and
appreciating the ways in which God is dealing with you.

The testing through which you are going is part of your learning to persevere. When we first become Christians our understanding of the manner in which God works is small. As we progress, so our understanding and appreciation of God's ways with us grow. When Paul wrote to the Thessalonians he was full of thankfulness to God for their salvation. He marks out the beginning of that grace for all believers: not when we became Christians, but in eternity when God the Father set his love on us and chose us for salvation. Paul reflects on the ultimate purpose of that grace, 'the obtaining of the glory of our Lord Jesus Christ'. This is nothing less than the glory Christ possesses and shares with all his redeemed people in the world to come. Paul gives thanks for the means that God has chosen by which we will reach that goal God has purposed: the Spirit's work of holiness in our hearts and 'belief in the truth'. Your conversion to Christ and the holiness of life that follows are the consequence of God working in your heart.

You became a Christian when God called you through his gospel. Paul had reminded the Thessalonians of the day they heard the message of Christ—how it came to them in power. When they received the Word of God, which they first heard from Paul, they welcomed it as a message from God and not from men (1 Thes. 1:5; 2:13). The call of God to salvation is effective and draws us in to begin to enjoy all the purposes of grace in our Lord

Jesus Christ, beginning with eternal election in Christ and ending with sharing his glory in heaven.

There is a logical conclusion to all this. Instead of being shaken by all the troubles and sorrows that have threatened to overwhelm you, Paul says, 'stand fast' (2 Thes. 2:15a). It is a call to perseverance in the light of God's eternal love. Your afflictions cannot extinguish the great love of God towards you in Jesus Christ. The death of your husband has not caused any changes in the everlasting purposes and love of God. In fact, if your husband was a Christian, then his death has taken him even closer to that final glory, for he is now 'with Christ, which is far better' (Phil. 1:23). Your sense of loss is intense but your husband has entered into glory ahead of you. You sorrow, but not 'as others who have no hope' (1 Thes. 4:13). It would be contrary to Christ's purpose to reverse the plan of his salvation and rob your husband of the joy that is now his. Remember, before long you too will be with Christ and share in that glory.

How easily our anguish and distress blot out God's love for us! They descend like a dark thunder-cloud on a rainy day. They cause us to distrust his love. Our confidence in and love towards him tend to wane, and we are inclined to murmur, to struggle, and to fret, instead of believing in his all-wise providence and continuing to trust in our Saviour, Jesus Christ. The gospel teaches us to take refuge in God, to commit all our cares and concerns to our heavenly Father, and to submit to his ways with us. Sorrow, loss, and death are among the worst things we experience now, sin excepted. One day, none of these things will trouble us any more.

The gospel does not minimize the reality of your grief. You are now alone, you have lost your husband. No two people will experience the same degree of grief. That experience depends on so many factors. However, it is often a shattering blow that affects your thoughts, feelings, and behaviour. It may mean that you lose your bearings, especially in the acute phase of grief in the first few months. You may be numb with shock, or a hundred and one concerns may be rushing through your head and you are not sure whether you are 'coming or going'. You discover how difficult it is to accept what has happened. Your hold on God has perhaps been severely shaken as a consequence. In the light of what Paul says about your salvation, even though your faith has been shaken, God's hold on you has never been stronger. His purposes of salvation cannot fail—neither for you nor for your husband. Everything God the Father is in his wisdom, love, power, and faithfulness, the Lord Jesus Christ also is. He also took our nature: he was 'a Man of sorrows and acquainted with grief' (Isa. 53:3). He shared our earthly experiences, including our sufferings and heartaches. That means he is qualified to come to your aid, sympathize with you, and help you in your time of need (Heb. 4:15). It may sound trite, but you are never alone. In Jesus Christ,

God has wrapped his everlasting love around you. The Spirit of God is now your Comforter.

Perhaps you are reading this and you are not a Christian. Do not despair. Let me point you to the Saviour, Jesus Christ. Sorrow and loss are terrible things, but sin is a worse evil than everything else. Sin is against God. You are helpless in the face of sin and the penalty of sin, which is death. This 'Man of sorrows' came into a world of sin and sorrow where death reigned because of sin. Jesus Christ came to save sinners. He experienced great personal grief as he went to the cross, for there he endured the wrath of God against sin. He shed his blood out of love for sinners to secure the salvation from sin for all those who come to him. By his death in the place of sinners he purchased the forgiveness for sins. He then rose from the dead and conquered death itself.

A Christian is someone who trusts not a dead Saviour, but the risen and living Lord. Real comfort in grief is elusive. Ultimately it is not found in any human being. It is found only in Jesus Christ, who experienced grief, who overcame grief, who died, and who then conquered death itself. Jesus said, 'I am the bread of life. He who comes to Me shall never hunger, and he who believes in Me shall never thirst' (John 6:35). Have you come? Have you cast yourself as a lost and guilty sinner on the one and only Saviour? Do you now enjoy peace with God through Jesus Christ?

Chapter 18

A living hope

Blessed be the God and Father of our Lord Jesus Christ, who according to His abundant mercy has begotten us again to a living hope through the resurrection of Jesus Christ from the dead, to an inheritance incorruptible and undefiled and that does not fade away, reserved in heaven for you, who are kept by the power of God through faith for salvation ready to be revealed in the last time.
1 Peter 1:3–5

Grief in the face of death is real, both for a Christian believer and for an unbeliever. However, there is a very significant difference. A Christian possesses 'a living hope through the resurrection of Jesus Christ from the dead' (1 Peter 1:3b). As we have already seen, a Christian grieves but does not sorrow 'as others who have no hope' (1 Thes. 4:13–14). The Greek philosopher Aristotle sorrowed over death but without hope. Death, he said, is a terrible thing, it is the end. All his human wisdom could not provide any hope in the face of death.

The distinctive Christian hope is real because Jesus Christ has risen from the dead. We know this because it is a matter of divine revelation that lies at the heart of the gospel. Jesus plainly declared the facts and also promised, 'This is the will of the Father who sent Me, that of all He has given Me I should lose nothing, but should raise it up at the last day. And this is the will of Him who sent Me, that everyone who sees the Son and believes in Him may have everlasting life; and I will raise him up at the last day' (John 6:39–40).

There are so many other verses in the Bible that speak of this hope. Some of them were written in times of great trial and affliction, when persecution was stretching the faith of Christians to its limits. In such circumstances they needed strong encouragement if they were to stand firm. So Peter told his readers who were 'grieved by various trials' (1 Peter 1:6) that there was a heavenly inheritance reserved in heaven for believers in Christ. It was kept for them by God, and they were being kept by God's power through faith, so that it was impossible for them to lose this salvation in Christ. He went on to speak of a 'joy inexpressible and full of glory' as he contemplated the full salvation yet to be experienced (v. 8). No wonder that he began with words of praise to God in verse 3!

Paul testified to the Corinthians, some of whom were questioning resurrection from the dead, that 'Christ is risen from the dead, and has become the firstfruits of those who have fallen asleep … each one in his own order: Christ the firstfruits, afterward those who are Christ's at His coming' (1 Cor. 15:20, 23). His picture language is clear. There is a 'resurrection harvest' taking place. The harvest has already begun. Christ is like the firstfruits and has already been gathered safely. He is in glory. The rest of the harvest—those who have believed on Christ—will be gathered in when he returns for them at his coming. One of the reasons why we experience bereavement is to ripen us for the harvest. The Lord Jesus is jealous for our love and would have us long more for him and for heaven. Fasten your hold on Christ and his promises. Let your love for him abound.

No Christian is to adopt a 'whatever-will-be-will-be' attitude. That is not godly submission. It is a form of fatalism that leaves you cold and comfortless. Stoicism that says you must repress your emotions produces the same effects. The gospel tells us that we can face the reality of death, and the consequences of grief and loneliness that death inevitably brings, with the reality of Christ's promises and Christ's triumph over death. All who belong to Christ will be raised from the dead at the coming of Christ. Some have 'fallen asleep' (the Bible's way of describing the death of believers) ahead of others and are already with Christ. No one will be left behind on the great day. All the dead will be raised from the dead and those alive will be caught up with them to meet the

Lord in the air. In this way 'we shall always be with the Lord' (1 Thes. 4:17).

Two questions remain, and I am often asked them, not only by those who have been bereaved, but also by married men and women. The first question arises from the words of Jesus in Matthew 22:30, that 'in the resurrection they neither marry nor are given in marriage'. Those who ask want to know whether a husband and his wife will meet again in heaven if there is no marriage. But what kind of a hope would it be, I would ask, if you were to think that your husband would mean no more to you than other redeemed people in heaven? That, I believe, would be too cruel to even contemplate.

The Lord Jesus tells us that marriage will no longer be fitting for the state of glory. From our Lord's words in Matthew 22:30 we conclude that marriage, as we know it here, will not exist, and so a husband will no longer need his wife as a helper and a husband will no longer need to cherish and nourish his wife. Furthermore, no children will be born in heaven.

The Lord Jesus Christ will be the chief source of our joy and comfort in glory. Those who have believed on him will be perfectly and permanently holy and happy, both in their bodies and in their spirits. However, that does not mean that the relationships you had in this life will count for nothing in heaven. If you once enjoyed the companionship of a Christian husband, you can be certain that your companionship will continue in heaven, but it will not be marriage. It is scarcely conceivable that Christ would ignore a relationship that he had established and blessed in the first place. Marriage was ordained by God from the very beginning. Nevertheless, in glory the relationship will take on different dimensions. Speaking of our loved ones, Edward Donnelly helpfully explains, 'you will know them more intimately, love them more intensely, delight in them more fully … We can look at Christians whom we love especially and praise God that we will continue to love them, more and more, for ever and ever.'[1] John Frame agrees with him when he says, 'I don't know exactly what will replace sexual pleasure, but I know that our intimacy with God and with one another will be something greater and better than anything we know and enjoy on this earth—as everything will be!'[2]

This living hope remains, therefore, as the source of our comfort. Death and the separation caused by death do not diminish our hope in any way. Believers are to comfort one another and to build one another up with the words of hope. At the same time, we have to admit that we do not have all the answers to the questions that puzzle us. It is always true that it is Christ who with great tenderness and sympathy binds up our wounds, yet we must confess that we cannot measure the ways of Almighty God. We experience the ways and workings of God and he brings sorrows into our lives. His wisdom and his purposes in these sorrows remain hidden from us. He owes us no explanations. He created the world in wisdom and power long before we his creatures were born. We must humble ourselves before him, acknowledge that he, and he alone, is God, and learn to trust him.

It should be clear from the above that reunion with loved ones will not be our greatest joy in heaven—the Lord Jesus Christ will. That has a bearing on the second question I am sometimes asked, namely, 'What comfort can there be for me as my husband never believed in Christ?' Comfort in these distressing circumstances comes from directly trusting in Christ. I do not know precisely how this comfort will be created in us, but I do know that God undertakes to make all things new. He promises a new heaven and a new earth in Revelation 21:1–7. There, in verse 4, God promises 'to wipe away every tear' from our eyes. Not only will death be banished, but sorrow, crying, and pain will no longer be part of our experience. That includes, I believe, the griefs and sorrows that arise because of the loss of an unconverted husband. In ways we do not yet understand, the joy of having God as our God will swallow up all other sorrows.

Samuel Rutherford often wrote to grieving friends. He told them to lay their hands on their mouths and not constantly ask the Lord why he had removed a husband, a wife, or a child and brought such distress on them. Rather, they should ask who had done this and seek grace to submit to his sovereignty. 'If it be from the Lord ... it is enough.'[3] That is godly submission. May the Lord grant you that same spirit as you imbibe the wisdom of God's care for the widow.

ENDNOTES

Introduction

1 Andrew A. Bonar, *Diary and Life* (Edinburgh: Banner of Truth, 1960), pp. 226–227.

2 Donald Howard, *Christians Grieve Too* (Edinburgh: Banner of Truth, 1980). It has been frequently reprinted.

3 C. S. Lewis, *A Grief Observed* (London: Faber & Faber, 1961). This has also been frequently republished.

4 Albert N. Martin, *Gleanings from a Grieving Heart*, 14, 21, 28 November 2004. These sermons are available from Trinity Baptist Church, Montville, New Jersey, USA, or may be heard at: sermonaudio.com. Subsequently, the substance of the sermons was produced in a small booklet, *Godly Grieving: Gleanings from a Pastor's Heart*, which is also available from Trinity Baptist Church.

Ch. 2 God relieves the widow

1 'Lifts up' comes from the same word that is translated 'relieves' in Ps. 146:9.

Ch. 5 Submitting to God's wise ways

1 John Newton, 'Begone, Unbelief', 1779.

Ch. 12 Omnipotent compassion

1 Faith Cook, *Samuel Rutherford and his Friends* (Edinburgh: Banner of Truth, 1992), p. 6.

2 See, for example, Isa. 1:17, 23; 10:1–2; Jer. 7:6–7; 22:3; Ezek. 22:6–8; and Micah 6:6–8.

Ch. 16 Younger widows

1 According to Numbers 30:9, the widow would be under obligation to keep such a vow. Perhaps Paul was also trying to protect such a young widow from a life of unhappiness and misery, because she might be making a vow without realizing what she was really undertaking to do. Paul was thinking much further ahead than a young, emotionally distressed widow would be able to do, and he showed special pastoral sensitivity at this point. A widow burdened with a sense of being unfulfilled could easily be tempted to become bitter and resentful. To be on a list of widows in such a state would have serious consequences, both for the church and for the widow herself.

Ch. 18 A living hope

1 Edward Donnelly, *Biblical Teaching on the Doctrines of Heaven and Hell* (Edinburgh: Banner of Truth, 2001), pp. 119–120. I would recommend the entire book but especially the final chapter.

2 John M. Frame, *Salvation Belongs to the Lord: An Introduction to Systematic Theology* (New Jersey: P&R, 2006), p. 293.

3 Andrew A. Bonar, (ed.), *Letters of Samuel Rutherford* (4th edn.; Edinburgh and London: Oliphant, Anderson & Ferrier, 1891), p. 628. I would recommend a reading of Rutherford's letters, especially those written for the bereaved. They are full of wise and comforting counsel, 'strong meat' for the believer.

TOPICAL INDEX OF SCRIPTURE REFERENCES TO WIDOWS

The following passages relating to widows have been placed in their context.

God and widows in the Old Testament

GOD THE DEFENDER OF THE WIDOW

Deuteronomy 10:17–19
Psalm 68:4–6
Psalm 94:1–7
Proverbs 15:25

GOD'S PROVISION FOR THE WIDOW

Deuteronomy 16:10–15
Deuteronomy 24:18–22
Deuteronomy 25:4–6
Deuteronomy 26:11–14
Psalm 146:5–10

GOD'S PROVISION FOR SPECIFIC WIDOWS

Naomi and Ruth: Ruth 1–4
Elijah and the widow in Zarephath: 1 Kings 17:8–24 (see also Luke 4:25–26)
Elisha and the widow's oil: 2 Kings 4:1–7

God's warnings against oppressing widows

IN THE LAW

Exodus 22:21–24
Deuteronomy 24:16–18
Deuteronomy 27:19

Care for the widow a part of godliness

Job 29:12–14

Job 31:17–19 (see also Job 22:8–10; 24:3, 21)

James 1:26–27

FAMILY RESPONSIBILITIES FOR WIDOWS

1 Timothy 5:3–8, 16

THE CHURCH'S CARE FOR WIDOWS

Acts 6:1–6

Dorcas: Acts 9:36–43

1 Timothy 5:3–16 (esp. vv. 3, 9–10, 16)